Alaska

D0004960

AMERICA THE BEAUTIFUL

Second Series

Alaska

·····································

Donna Walsh Shepherd

Children's Press®
A Division of Scholastic Inc.
New York Toronto London Auckland Sydney
Mexico City New Delhi Hong Kong
Danbury, Connecticut

Frontispiece: Totem pole in Sitka National Park

Front cover: Sitka Harbor

Back cover: Denali National Park

Consultant: Jo Antonsson, State Historian, Alaska Historical Society

Please note: All statistics are as up-to-date as possible at the time of publication.

Book production by Editorial Directions, Inc.

Library of Congress Cataloging-in-Publication Data

Walsh Shepherd, Donna.
　　Alaska / by Donna Walsh Shepherd
　　　p. cm. — (America the beautiful. Second series)
　　Includes bibliographical references and index.
　　Summary : Describes the geography, history, economy and industry, natural
resources, arts and recreation, and people of the state of Alaska.
　　ISBN 0-516-20992-2
　　1. Alaska—Juvenile literature. [1. Alaska.] I. Title. II. Series.
F904.3.W26 1999
979.8—dc21   96-15297
　　　　　　　　　　　　　　　　　　　　　　　　　　　　　　　　　　　　　CIP
　　　　　　　　　　　　　　　　　　　　　　　　　　　　　　　　　　　　　AC

©1999 by Children's Press, A Division of Scholastic Inc.
All rights reserved. Published simultaneously in Canada
Printed in Mexico.
　6 7 8 9 10 R 08 07 06 05

Acknowledgments

Many thanks to all those who shared their expertise with me, including the terrific librarians at Loussac Library's Alaska Collection, especially Bruce Merrill; the Alaska Tourism Marketing Council; Joanne Welch of the Alaska Public Lands Information Office; Mike Zacharof, who survived the Aleut internment as a child; Kevin Waring, economist; Dr. Margritt Engel, Steller expert; Julie Stoneking, Sage Stoneking-Sundown, and Diane Paukan, for help with the Scammon Bay section; Nick Roghair, of Barrow; my father, Maurice Walsh, biologist and naturalist; my son Chad Shepherd, sports journalist; and my dear husband, Morris Shepherd, who can really come through in a pinch at both the stove and the computer.

Anchorage

Mount Megeik Volcano

Aurora borealis

Contents

Ketchikan

Snowmobiling

Alaska pipeline

Yup'ik Inuit

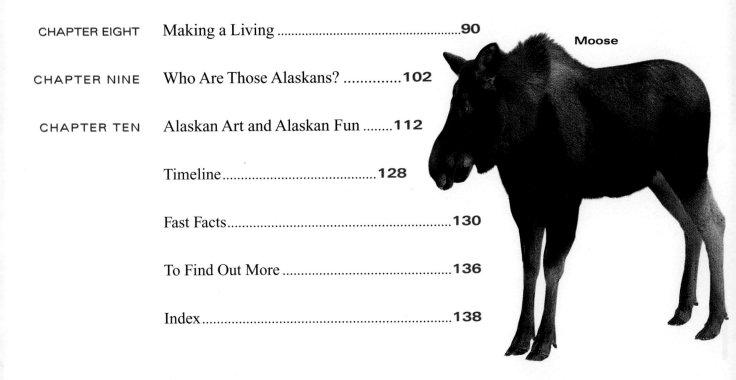

Moose

CHAPTER ONE

Alaska—A Great Land

The town of Kotzebue at midnight during the summer

On a bright summer's night, the sun sets leisurely in the northern sky. Before the last pink light of sunset fades, the first pink rays of sunrise wash over the northern horizon beside it. Salmon fill the streams. Caribou graze across the tundra. Berries ripen all across the lush land. Vegetables grow to mythical size. At midnight, people still enjoy the evening. Children play ball in the streets, neighbors visit or head for their favorite fishing stream or read a book—all by sunlight.

On a bright winter's morning, the sun slowly rises over the southern mountain crest and turns the shadowy world below to brilliance. The crystal white world captures the sun's light and mirrors it back to the turquoise sky. Hoarfrost ice crystals growing on every tree fracture the first light into a rainbow of diamonds. Birds flirt around a long-legged moose crunching step by step through the crusty snow. In a few hours, the winter sun will set below the southern horizon. Even in the darkness, the white world glows under a net of millions of stars, and the northern lights race across the sky. In the winter glow, people ski along quiet wooded trails, fish through ice holes for lake trout, and sled in the crisp, clean night air.

Alaska is a land of contrasts and extremes, of rare beauty and

Opposite: Sunrise over Mount McKinley in the Denali National Park

big distances. It's the largest state by far, but it's the second least populated. It's one of the two newest states, but it was the first place populated in North America. Although a third of Alaska lies above the Arctic Circle, the Aleutian Islands nearly reach the same latitude as Seattle. Anchorage is due north of Hawaii. Mainland Alaska comes within a few miles of Russia.

The state covers so much area that it has both temperate rain forests and frozen deserts. Extreme winter snow measurements have varied from 3 inches (7.6 cm) to 1,000 feet (305 m). Alaska has Mount McKinley, the highest point in North America, as well as the Aleutian Trench, where the Pacific Plate folds under the North American plate, setting off volcanoes and earthquakes. The Aleutian Trench is nearly as deep as Mount McKinley is high.

In the cities, such as Anchorage, there are world-class hotels, restaurants, arts centers, and plenty of stoplights. In the remote villages, people still keep many traditions of their ancestors. Some small villages don't even have cars. Few roads connect town to town. Much of the travel throughout the state is by plane.

Alaska is a land so rich in natural resources that the fight for control of those resources has shaped much of Alaska's history and continues to shape its future. It has tremendous stores of animal and mineral resources—such as furs, gold, fish, timber, coal, oil, and zinc—that have fueled international commerce. Yet, what can't be sold may be more valuable. So little of Alaska has been severely altered by the presence of humankind that Alaska is one of the few great expanses of natural land left in the country. In Alaska, there is an empty vastness in every vista—mountains, oceans, valleys, lakes, glaciers.

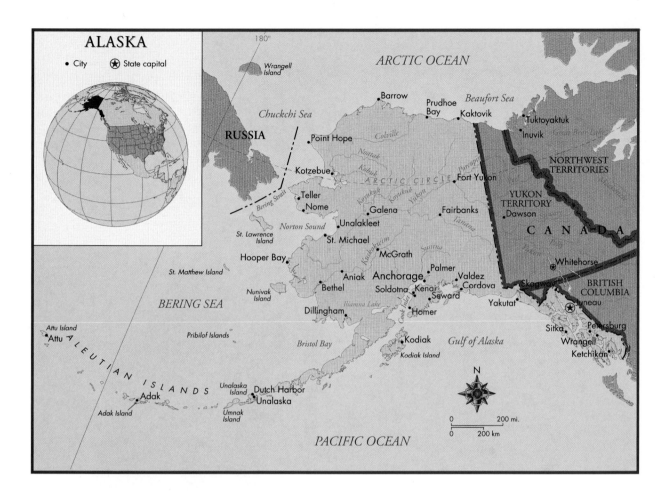

Geopolitical map of Alaska

Alaska is a land of special places, special moments, and special people. But it is not a tender land. Since humans first walked across the land bridge from Asia, only the most hardy have felt at home in Alaska. Only the strong of body and spirit have thrived in this place where temperatures have ranged from 100°F (38°C) to −80°F (−62°C). Life in Alaska has different rhythms than life in other states. The days seem to contract in the cold winter and expand in the warm summer. But they are always interesting days and no matter the season, they often begin with the most colorful sunrises and end with the most brilliant sunsets.

CHAPTER TWO

Coming to the New Continent

About 7,000 years ago, people left their homes in Asia and walked east. The winters blew colder then. Summers held little warmth against winter's ice. The polar ice cap and mountain glaciers grew larger and thicker as each summer couldn't melt the previous winter's snows. With no melting snows to replenish the northern oceans, more ocean water became locked into ice each year. Land between Asia and Alaska, once 300 feet (91 m) underwater, had appeared. Animals crossed back and forth over this land bridge, and Asian people followed them to North America.

A caribou grazes on rich summer tundra just as they might have thousands of years ago.

When this gathering of people reached the mainland of North America, they did not turn south as their ancestors had thousands of years earlier, following an ice-free corridor along the Yukon Valley and down the Rocky Mountains.

Instead, these newcomers followed the coast and turned north into the cold. Today, this land is considered one of the harshest places to live in the world. But then, the people saw great abundance: seas filled with fish and sea mammals, land covered with berries in the summer, lakes full of nesting birds. They called this new place home. The Aleuts, the people of the Aleutian Island Chain, called it *Alyeska*—the great land. *Alaska* comes from that name, and it still means the Great Land.

Opposite: An Inuit man hunting with his harpoon

Settling the New World

Alaska is believed to be the first point settled in the Western Hemisphere. Asian tribespeople first crossed land that formerly had been underwater to reach the Western Continent 25,000 to 40,000 years ago during the ice age. They were probably nomads following animals such as the woolly mammoth, mastodon, saber-toothed tiger, steppe bison, antelope, moose, camel, lion, caribou, and musk ox.

Over several thousand years, their descendants slowly moved into Canada, the mainland United States, and eventually down into Mexico and Central and South America. The Athabascan Indians of central Alaska share a similar language with the Navajo Indians of the Southwest. ■

The Early People

For thousands of years, Alaskan Natives—the Aleuts; the Yup'ik and Inupiat Inuit of the western and northern coasts; the Athabascan Indians of the interior; and the Tlingit and Haida Indians of southeastern Alaska—lived on the abundance of the land and sea. Some years were good. Other years, starvation and deadly weather became neighbors.

Native Alaskans were one of the few Native peoples of the world whose diet was not based on a starch such as bread or rice. They ate mostly seal, whale, fish, caribou, and moose. Berries, birds, and eggs added variety in the summer. Sometimes squirrel, rabbit, bear, and walrus provided nourishment. Even today, these foods are an important part of Native life. In some areas, they provide 70 percent of people's protein. Spring and late summer, then as now, were busy times of harvesting and preserving foods. Winter was for carving and making clothes, for dancing and storytelling.

Opposite: Native Alaskans

Traditional Native Homes

Alaskan Natives never lived in igloos—ice houses—except during emergencies when traveling. The Inuit and Aleuts lived in homes called *barabaras* (above), built partly underground with whale ribs or driftwood logs as supports. They covered these supports with grass mats, moss, dried grasses, and soil. Bedding consisted of soft furs on platforms along the walls. The Aleuts had secret side rooms for hiding their children in times of danger. The barabaras were warm, comfortable, and often quite large.

The nomadic Athabascans built easily movable tepee-style homes with supports of birch saplings. They covered these with thick, warm caribou skins.

The Tlingit and Haida Indians lived in large wooden homes divided into compartments for each family with central cooking and meeting areas. They slept on platform beds covered with soft evergreen boughs.

Some Native people lived in these types of homes until the middle part of this century. Now everyone lives in more modern housing. ■

The Visitors

In the eighteenth century, Europeans were eager to explore the world and find a short trade route to Asia. They were convinced that surely America would have a waterway through it to the Pacific. At the same time, the Russian czar Peter the Great wanted to know more about the 6,000-mile (9,656-km) wilderness east of St. Petersburg. He assigned Vitus Bering to map Russia's eastern coastline and north Pacific Ocean.

In 1728, after traveling overland across Russia, Bering and his crew built two ships and sailed through the waterway separating Asia and North America, now known as the Bering Strait. This water covers what used to be the land bridge. However, it was too foggy for Bering to see North America and make accurate maps.

Bering returned in 1741 with scientists, artists, and naturalist George Steller. This time, Bering did find land. Steller and his shipmates went ashore for fresh water and found a Native camp empty of people, but with smoldering fires. Knowing the people must be watching from the forest, they took a few items from the camp and left iron pots and gifts from the ship. Bering claimed all the land for the Russian czar.

On the return trip to Russia, Bering became lost in very bad weather and ran short of food and fresh water. During a November storm, he and his crew shipwrecked on an island 400 miles (644 km) from

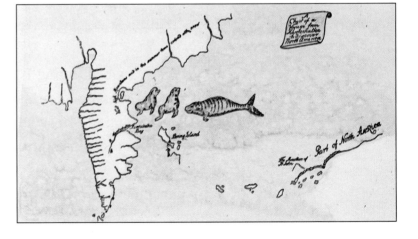

Peter the First of Russia

From a chart drawn in 1741 by a member of Vitus Bering's expedition

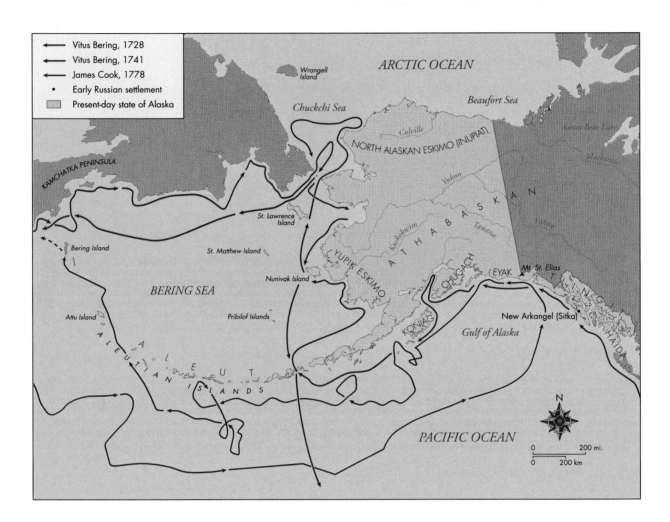

Map labels: ARCTIC OCEAN, Wrangell Island, Beaufort Sea, Great Bear Lake, Chuckchi Sea, Colville, NORTH ALASKAN ESKIMO (INUPIAT), Mackenzie, KAMCHATKA PENINSULA, Yukon, ATHABASKAN, St. Lawrence Island, Kuskokwim, Tanana, Yukon, Bering Island, St. Matthew Island, YUPIK ESKIMO, CHUGACH, EYAK, Mt. St. Elias, BERING SEA, Nunivak Island, KONIAG, New Arkangel (Sitka), TLINGIT, Attu Island, Pribilof Islands, Gulf of Alaska, ALEUTIAN ISLANDS, HAIDA, PACIFIC OCEAN, N, 0 200 mi., 0 200 km

Exploration of Alaska

Siberia, now named Bering Island. Bering and many of his men died there of scurvy and disease. Bering never knew the role he played in opening Alaska and the North Pacific. In the summer, the survivors built a small ship from the wreckage and sailed back to Russia.

Among the information and samples they brought back were sea otter furs more luxurious than any the Russians had ever seen.

Knowing the Chinese would pay high prices for such furs, traders and fur merchants quickly headed to the new Russian territory.

In America, under Alexander Baranof, the Russian governor, the Russians enslaved the Alaskan Natives to work as hunters. Often they kidnapped Aleut hunters, sometimes starving them to force them to work. Some Aleuts were taken as far away as California. With their ships full of furs, the Russians sailed home, leaving the Aleuts to make it through the winter on their own. Each spring, the Russians returned, demanding more furs from those who survived. In 1741, when Bering's party landed, there were more than 20,000 Aleuts. By 1800, because of cruel treatment and disease, only 2,000 to 2,500 were left.

In the 1790s, missionaries followed the fur traders to Russian America. Aghast at how poorly the Native people were treated, they protested to the czar and treatment improved.

As word of the Russian exploration and trading spread, Spain, England, and France sent explorers to the North Pacific. England sent Captain James Cook to find an ice-free waterway from the Atlantic to the Pacific. In 1778, Cook sailed up the American northwest coast, creating the first reliable charts. He sailed into the Chukchi Sea before running into impassable ice. From there, he sailed south to chart the Aleutian Islands and on to the Hawaiian Islands, where he was killed by natives.

Captain James Cook

George Steller

George Steller, a German physician and naturalist, accompanied Bering on the second voyage to Alaska and was the first known European to stand on Alaskan soil. He was very intelligent and knowledgeable but not appreciated by some of the crew. Those who took his advice on eating certain types of seaweed and plants to prevent scurvy survived. He studied and recorded many unknown species of animals and birds, including the Steller jay, the Steller sea lion, and the now extinct Steller sea cow. ■

A New Owner for Alyeska

By the mid 1850s, over-hunting made fur trading less profitable. The territory was sapping Russia of precious money and giving little in return. After heavy expenses in the Crimean War, Russia offered to sell Alaska to the United States in 1854.

Thirteen years later, William Seward, U.S. secretary of state and the driving force behind the purchase, signed papers at 4 A.M. on March 30, 1867, buying Alaska for $7.2 million dollars—2 cents an

Historical map of Alaska

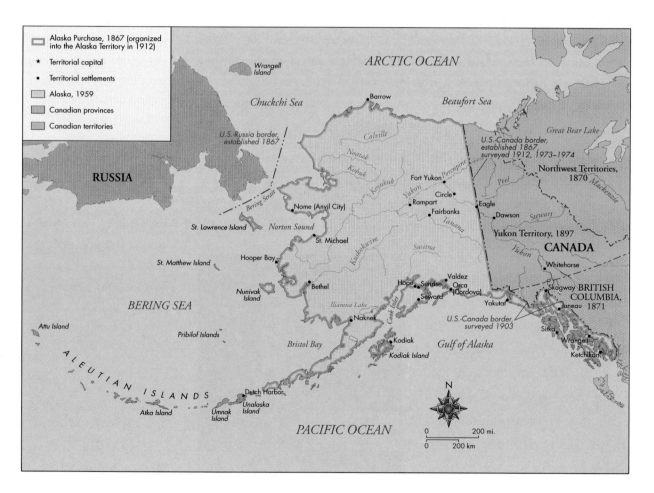

acre. The Russians were elated to get what they considered such a high price. Some Americans were less elated. Newspaper cartoons and editorials called Alaska SEWARD'S FOLLY and SEWARD'S ICEBOX. But Seward always felt that buying Alaska was the best thing he ever did and that eventually the whole country would realize it.

In Sitka on October 18, 1867, the Russians slowly lowered their flag. Halfway down it stuck. A Russian soldier climbed the flagpole to cut it down while Princess Maria Maksoutov, wife of the gover-

Sitka, or New Archangel, as it might have looked in 1869

William H. Seward

William Seward was a New York lawyer and politician, serving as governor and U.S. senator. Abraham Lincoln appointed him as secretary of state. Seward worked against slavery, to keep foreign governments out of the war between the states, and to expand the territory of the United States. Seward visited Alaska in 1869 and took great pleasure in addressing the assembled people at Sitka as "Citizens of Alaska, fellow citizens of the United States." ∎

nor, wept. The U.S. flag was raised, and Russian America was gone. Alaska became a U.S. possession under the protection of the U.S. Army.

Seward was indeed a visionary. His "folly" turned out to be some of the richest land in the world: first in furs, fish, and whales, then in gold and copper, now in minerals like oil, coal, zinc, and natural gas. Alyeska is a great land indeed.

Remnants of the Russian heritage remain today. Many places hold the names given them by the Russians. Many families have Russian surnames, especially Aleut families. The Russian Ortho-

A Russian Orthodox Church in the Aleutian Islands

The Pribilof Islands

Russian fur merchants brought the Aleuts to the uninhabited Pribilof Islands in the Bering Sea to hunt fur seals. They were left there to survive as best they could. The tundra covered volcanic rock outcroppings are far from land. The outcroppings serve as a rest stop and breeding grounds for millions of migratory birds and sea mammals. The seas are rich in fish, shellfish, and plankton. St. Paul Island, the largest, measures only 8 by 14 miles (13 by 23 km).

In summer, the green tundra blooms thick with wildflowers and berries. All around, nearly everything else is blue sky and sea. Walking along the cliffs, one hears birds call and seals bellow. Nesting sea birds—puffins, murres, cormoronts, kittiwakes, and auklets crowd every crook and ledge of the rocky cliffs. Once again, the beaches below are jammed thick with fur seals—the beachmasters, their harem and pups. Blue fox trot everywhere, but a herd of reindeer brought to the island 100 years ago remains elusive.

Today, on the slopes of a protected bay, the community of St. Paul overlooks the sea. At the nearby harbor the Aleuts provide services for the international fishing fleets. In the heart of town and of the island's people is the Russian Orthodox St. Peter and Paul Church. ■

dox religion remains important in southern and western Alaska. Now, more than 250 years after Bering landed, once again trade flourishes between Alaska and Russia.

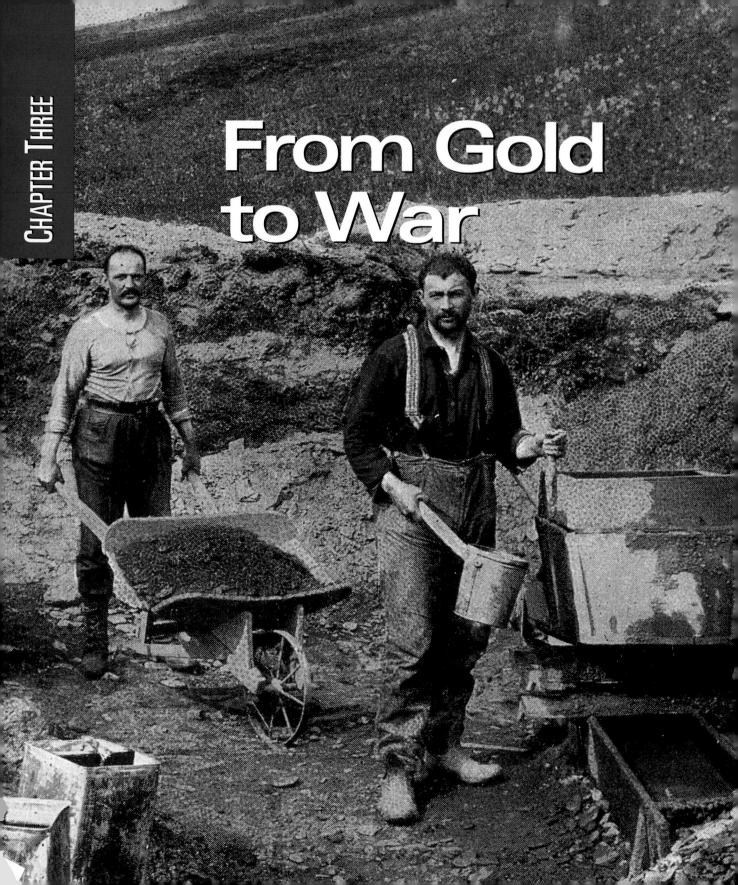

CHAPTER THREE

From Gold to War

In the second half of the nineteenth century, the United States was busy with the aftermath of the American Civil War and the movement into the West. Alaska was put on a back burner and ignored. The future state suffered under uninterested military control. In 1877, the military left, leaving Alaska with customs agents and three postmasters as its only government officials.

One of a few laws Congress passed between 1867 and 1884 that concerned Alaska turned the Pribilof Islands fur seal breeding grounds into a reserve. Finally in 1884, Congress passed the Organic Act of Alaska officially giving Alaska a governor, a code of laws, court personnel, and a school system.

Cover of *The Klondike News*, April 1, 1898

People Begin Heading North

Slowly, more and more people came into the new territory—prospectors, adventurers, traders, and merchants. The first official census was done in 1880. Of the 33,426 people living year-round in Alaska, 430 were white, 6 black, and the rest native. In 1879, among the curious who came was naturalist John Muir. The state's grand beauty and massive glaciers captivated him. He wrote the book *Travels in Alaska* and articles about Alaska for San Francisco newspapers. Partially because of Muir's influence, regularly sched-

Opposite: Mining on the Seward Peninsula in 1901

uled boats sailed up Alaska's Inside Passage in summers. Once in Alaska, people traveled primarily by river in summers and dogsled in winter. There were no roads.

Discovering Gold

In 1848, gold was discovered in California. People rushed to the West Coast. As gold became difficult to find, miners began drifting north because of rumors of gold in Alaska. But there were more than just rumors: The gold was there. Russia knew that when it sold Alaska to the United States. A Russian engineer had found gold in south central Alaska the same year as the great gold discovery in California. But a bit of gold was of little concern to the Russians compared to the valuable fur trade, so the engineer's report was ignored.

The big gold find that brought Alaska to national attention didn't happen in Alaska at all but in Canada. On August 17, 1896, while washing dishes in a tributary of the Klondike River, George Carmack and his Indian partners Skookum Jim and Tagish Charlie found gold layered "like cheese in a sandwich," Carmack later said.

A gold nugget from the Crow Creek Mine near Anchorage

It took a year for word of the remote discovery to reach the United States. The world was in a deep economic depression. In July 1897, sixty-eight ragged miners stepped off ships returning from Alaska to San Francisco and Seattle. They carried sacks full of gold, boxes full of gold, blankets full of gold. The world went wild. Everyone talked of heading

Gold Rush Characters

People from all walks of life came north to Alaska to make their fortunes. A fortunate few did by finding gold, others did in other ways. Big Alex McDonald made $20 million, but gave most of it to charity. Diamond Lil, a popular entertainer, had a diamond between her front teeth. Miner Swiftwater Bill Gates took baths in champagne.

Klondike Kate was able to save $150,000 from gold nuggets that miners threw during her vaudeville act. Belinda Mulroney threw her last half dollar into the Yukon River and vowed never to use small change again. She opened the most successful hotel in the North. Mattie Crosby crossed the Chilkoot Trail as a teenager. She ran a bathhouse in Flat and wrote articles about the gold rush and Alaska for a San Diego newspaper. She was one of many African-Americans to find adventure and a new life in Alaska.

Soapy Smith was Skagway's genuine Bad Guy and the last of the Wild West outlaws. Lee "China Joe" Hing was so kind-hearted he was said to be the only man in Alaska without an enemy. Others who came north included writer Jack London, poet Robert Service, and photographer E. A. Hegg. ■

north to make their fortune. Magazines sent reporters and photographers to cover the story. More than 100,000 people actually set out for the Klondike River. As people poured into the north, they made major new gold strikes across Alaska. In 1899, the Three Lucky Swedes discovered gold in Nome. In 1902, Felix Pedro discovered the first of several rich deposits around Fairbanks.

Many of those who came north stayed and opened businesses. Between 1890 and 1900, Alaska's population doubled to 63,592. More importantly, the people of the United States suddenly knew about Alaska. They knew where it was, what it was like, and that the land indeed had value.

Bush Pilots

After World War I, pilots looking for new horizons flew north. Alaska had almost no roads and took to the airplane immediately. Because there were few maps, pilots usually navigated by following rivers. Often they had to stop midtrip on a sandbar to refuel. The

A bush pilot picking up passengers

pilots flew people, goods, and mail all around the territory. Some-times they flew rescue and medical emergencies that put their own lives at risk.

Because Alaska's weather was unpredictable and dangerous, bush pilots got reputations for being fearless and lucky—those who survived. Harold Gilliam survived six crashes in 1931 alone. Don Sheldon told of flying at 120 miles (193 km) per hour by Mount McKinley and discovering the winds were so strong they were pushing him backwards. All pilots carried spare parts so they could fix their plane if it crashed. Many early pilots such as Noel Wien; Robert Reeve, "The Glacier Pilot"; and "Mudhole" Smith went on to establish the first airlines in the north. Airplanes are still a main source of transportation in Alaska.

Farming in the North

In 1935, during the Great Depression, to help develop Alaska, the U.S. government offered families a 40-acre (16-ha) farm for $5 an acre. In those hard times, many jumped at the chance for a fresh start. Two hundred families moved north to the rich wilderness land of the Matanuska Valley north of Anchorage to begin a new life.

They arrived in the rain to find none of the promised houses, barns, or schools. All rainy summer long, they lived in tents. Measles and scarlet fever ripped though the community. Many set-tlers left, too discouraged by summer's hardships to face the worse ones of winter. Others came to take their place.

During the next several years, short growing seasons and unpredictable weather often plagued the farmers. It was a tough

Growing alfalfa in Matanuska Valley

way to make a living. By 1948, only 40 of the original 202 families remained. Today, some of that land is still farmed by descendants of the original pioneer families.

World War II in the North

Alaska's next population boom came during World War II when the military expanded its presence in the north. Japan had bombed Hawaii and threatened to invade San Francisco. The Aleutian Islands are closer to Tokyo, San Francisco, and Seattle than Hawaii is. In June 1942, Japan attacked the Aleutian Islands, bombing Dutch Harbor and invading the uninhabited Attu and Kiska Islands. The military needed an overland way to get supplies north. President Roosevelt approved a road connecting Alaska to road systems in Canada and the United States.

The remains of a World War II Japanese freighter in Kiska

The building of the 1,519-mile (2,445-km)-long Alaska Highway from Dawson Creek, British Columbia, to Fairbanks, Alaska, through unsurveyed wild country in just more than eight months was a great feat of human willpower and resilience. Work crews, including many African-American troops, started at both the north and south ends of the proposed road. As guides walked through the forests and swamps hacking out a pathway with axes, bulldozers followed. They worked 16-hour days in –40°F (–40°C) weather or in mosquito-clouded summer humidity, lacking sufficient food, heat, and proper equipment.

One day near Kluane, Canada, the crew heading south heard crashing in the bushes. The soldiers grabbed their rifles. They had heard these sounds before. Was it a bear or a moose this time? No matter, it meant a bit of meat for a stew. But as they raised their rifles, guides from the northbound crew came into sight. Astounded, the soldiers dropped their rifles. Their job was done! They had created a winding lifeline to Alaska in an impossibly short eight months. Music, dancing, and singing lasted long into the night.

After moving thousands of troops to Alaska, the United States prepared to fight to regain the Attu and Kiska Islands in May 1943. Attu was a terrible battle. Finally, the U.S. troops took control. Rather than surrender, the Japanese soldiers committed suicide. Only 28 of more than 2,600 Japanese troops survived. Of the 11,000 American troops, 3,829 were injured or died.

To recapture Kiska, the United States bombed and shelled the island for more than two months. When troops finally came onshore, they discovered the 5,600 Japanese troops had escaped by ship in a heavy fog weeks earlier. The Japanese had held these islands for more than a year. Alaska became the only U.S. land ever to be occupied by a foreign government during war.

Aleut Internment

After Dutch Harbor was bombed, the American military decided to move the Aleuts from the Aleutian and Pribilof Islands. On June 14, 1942, ships showed up and took people away with no time to pack. Because the evacuation order was for Aleuts, white people living on the islands were allowed to stay. The military burned one village and moved troops into private homes in others.

The 881 Aleuts were moved to abandoned cannery buildings in southeastern Alaska without enough food, warmth, or medical care. People were so crowded, nearly everyone became sick. More

An abandoned prisoner of war camp on the Aleutian Islands

than eighty people, including many children, died that first year. At the nearby prisoner of war camp, the German prisoners received far better treatment, housing, food, and medical care than the Aleuts.

Most dispiriting to the Aleuts was the environment. They were people of treeless islands in the Pacific. At home, everywhere they looked was sea and sky. Most Aleuts had never seen a tree before. In the huge Sitka spruce and cedar forest, they felt trapped and smothered.

By law, only Aleuts are allowed to hunt fur seals. Because the government wanted the valuable seal oil and furs, 150 hunters were taken to the Pribilof Islands in the summers, leaving the women, children, and elderly alone for four months.

Finally, in August 1945, the military allowed the Aleuts to return to their islands. There the Aleuts found most of their villages and homes destroyed and looted. Even priceless religious icons had

The Chilkoot Trail

The Chilkoot Trail is part of the Klondike Gold Rush National Historical Park, which extends from Seattle to Dawson City in the Yukon Territory. The Chilkoot Trail starts near Skagway. Today, step by step, hikers follow the 33-mile (53-km)-long "Trail of Misery" the gold rushers took in 1898. After crossing the Chilkoot Mountains to Lake Bennett, the miners built rafts and floated more than 600 miles (966 km) down the Yukon River to the Klondike goldfields.

The miners climbed this steep and difficult trail about forty times in the dead of winter to carry their 2,000 pounds (907 kg) of supplies from Dyea or Skagway to Lake Bennett. The trail was so hard and cold that many discarded anything they decided was too heavy or unnecessary. Supplies, clothing, and the remains of the tent cities are still strewn along the entire trail. It has become an open museum in the forest. ■

St. Paul, one of the
Pribilof Islands

been stolen from the churches. This was done not by the enemy, but by the U.S. soldiers sent to protect the islands. All along the chain, the military left trash, oil spills, and live ammunition. For many years on this American land, there was no cleanup as there had been by the U.S. government in Europe and Japan.

The treatment of the Aleuts during the war was one of the worst violations of constitutional and human rights in modern U.S. history. Traditionally, Aleuts consider it disrespectful to complain, but when the Japanese Americans, who had also been interned, asked the Aleuts to join in a lawsuit against the government, they agreed. Finally, in 1988, the Aleuts received an apology and some monetary compensation for the damages from the U.S. government. They have invested the money and are using the earnings to restore their churches.

Chapter Four

North to the Future

ALASKA
STATEHOOD
1-3-1959
DWIGHT D. EISENHOWER

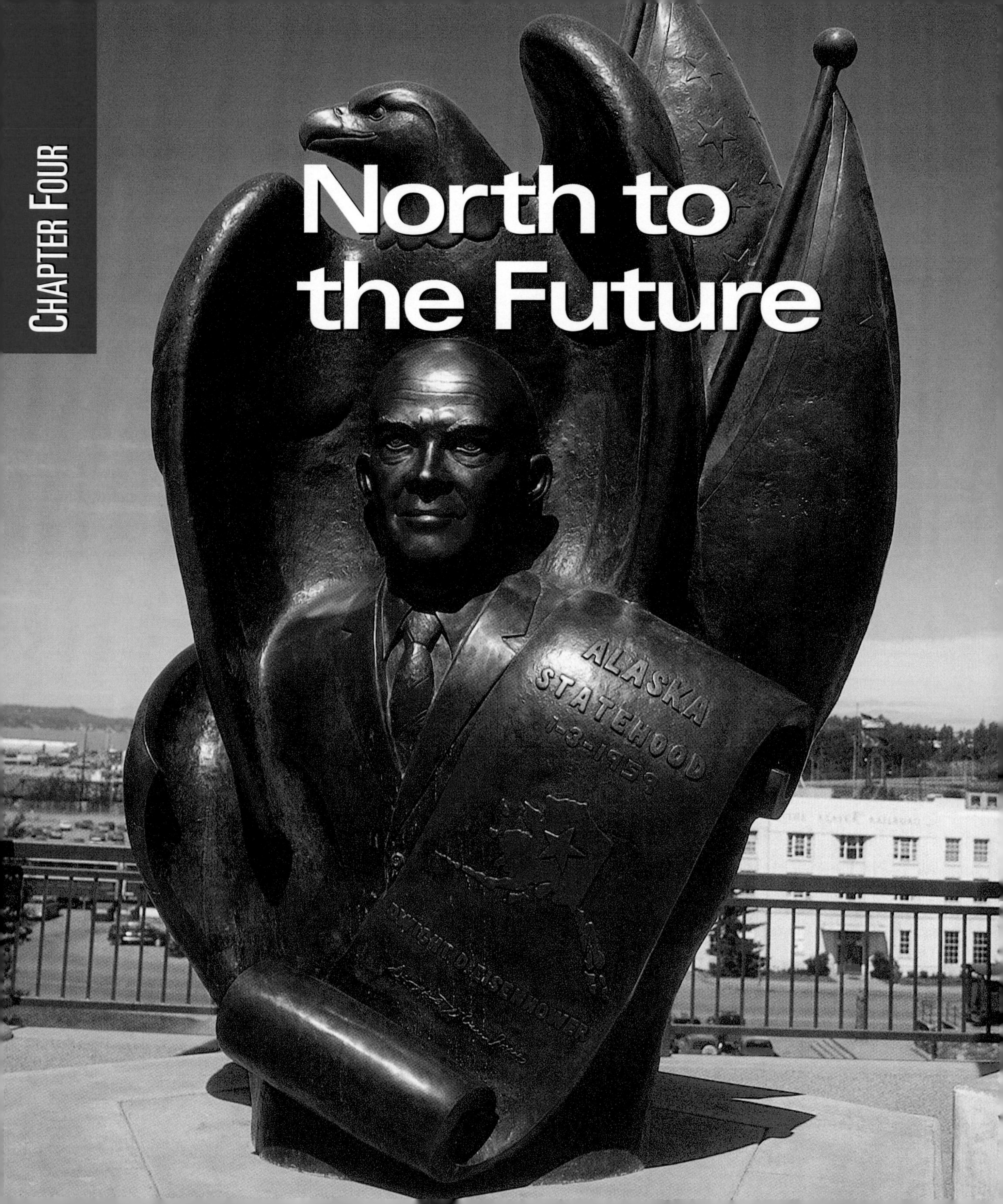

Alaskans gathering
to celebrate statehood

After World War II ended, Alaska's northern position remained vital to the United States. It was a time of distrust and hostilities with Russia, only 53 miles (85 km) from Alaska. As Russia tried to expand its influence in Asia, the U.S. military increased its presence in Alaska.

In the 1950s, former territorial governor Ernest Gruening, congressional delegate Bob Bartlett, and many other Alaskans worked to get statehood for Alaska. Among the opponents was the fishing industry based in Seattle, because as a state, Alaska would gain control of its own waters and resources. Committee after committee of Alaskans went to Washington, sometimes working jointly with Hawaiians who also wanted statehood. Finally, on June 30, 1958, the Alaska statehood bill passed both houses of Congress. President Eisenhower signed the bill on July 7. On January 3, 1959, Alaska officially became the forty-ninth state.

Who Gets What Land?

During the first few decades of Alaska's statehood, a land given to extremes swung from political complications to natural catastrophes to economic booms and back to start again.

The federal government gave Alaska the right to select 103.5

Opposite: A monument
to Alaska's statehood

We're In!

After World War II, Alaskan leaders began a campaign to familiarize Congress with Alaska's importance to the nation. In the early 1950s, several statehood bills passed the House of Representatives, but they always failed in the Senate. Finally, on June 30, 1958, statehood also passed the Senate, 64 votes to 20.

As the news spread, celebrations erupted across the state. People ran into the streets cheering and waving flags and signs. Honking cars, fire engines with sirens wailing, and jubilant crowds created instant parades. The citizens of Fairbanks sent a telegram thanking Congress for the vote. It became the world's longest telegram, as 2,200 people signed it. In Fairbanks, saloonkeeper Don Pearson decided to dye the Chena River gold. He and friends poured several packets of gold dye used for air rescues into the Chena. The entire town watched in amazement as the river turned not gold but pea green.

That August, 80 percent of the people of Alaska voted to accept statehood. The official ceremony took place in the White House on January 3, 1959, as President Dwight D. Eisenhower signed the proclamation making Alaska the forty-ninth state. At 9:15 A.M., the governor's office in Juneau received the call from the White House confirming the bill had been signed. At 9:18 A.M., territorial governor William Egan (left, with Bob Bartlett) was sworn in as the first state governor of Alaska. Alaska had come a long way since 1877 when customs agents and postmasters were in charge of the entire territory. ∎

million acres (42 million ha) of federal land as state land. The Alaskan Natives said the agreement ignored their rights to the land they had lived on for thousands of years. They formed the Alaska Federation of Natives to fight for their ancestral lands.

Shake, Rattle, and Roll

As these issues were being worked out, on Good Friday, March 27, 1964, everything was put aside with one giant jolt. At 5:36 P.M., as

The aftermath of Alaska's earthquake in 1964

people in Anchorage were heading home from work, cooking dinner, and enjoying the growing light and warmth of the coming spring, the earth moved. It moved so violently that people thought the world was ending. Roads ripped apart. Forests sank into the marshes, killing the trees. Marshes rose, killing the bog plants, animals, and salmon spawning areas. Flat land now looked like sand dunes. Trees grew out of the ground sideways.

People still tell earthquake stories of chandeliers swinging so violently that they bounced from side to side against the ceiling. They tell of rushing to the front door and watching the house across the street sink into the ground like a toy on a sieve of sand. Stories abound of wide cracks opening in the floor beneath their feet or of standing in a building and watching the outside wall fall off.

The energy released by the convulsing earth created a tsunami, a giant ocean wave. As the wall of water rushed toward the Prince William Sound coastal communities, people ran for high ground. When it hit, it tossed boats in the bay high onto the hillside. All of

Earthquake!

For five very long minutes on March 27, 1964, the earth jerked, waved, and seized. Initially the earthquake measured 8.6 on the Richter scale, but later, more accurate, measurements adjusted that to 9.2. It is the largest quake to ever hit North America and eighty times more powerful than the 1906 San Francisco earthquake. Each year about 1,000 earthquakes measuring 3.5 or stronger hit Alaska, the most earthquake-prone state. Since 1899, 80 quakes measured 7 or above. Quakes that strong are capable of severe damage. ■

Valdez was washed away. As the wave traveled across the ocean, people ran with bullhorns on Hawaii's beaches warning people to leave. Japan was put on alert. West Coast towns as far away as Crescent City, California, flooded. In all, 131 people were killed, very few considering the size of the quake. Most drowned in the tsunami.

The one thing the 1964 earthquake couldn't destroy was the people's spirit. With government loans, Anchorage rebuilt and Valdez relocated 4 miles (6 km) away on high ground. Even today when an especially strong earthquake hits, nearly everyone thinks of the Big One and wonders if this is another.

Fires added to Fairbanks's problems during the flood of 1967.

Water, Water, Everywhere

Only a few years later, Fairbanks had its own catastrophe. Fairbanks summers are normally dry and sunny, but not the summer of 1967. It rained all summer, saturating the ground. The second week of August started out sunny, but then it began pouring and pouring. Both roads into Fairbanks flooded on August 13. On August 14, people who thought they were safe went to bed to be awakened two hours later by evacuation sirens and water pouring into their homes. The entire Tanana Basin quickly flooded, and thousands of people were boated or helicoptered to the hilltop refugee center at the University of Alaska, Fairbanks. It took a week for the muddy Chena River to retreat into its banks.

Black Gold

Good things were happening in the state, too, though. Alaska had oil. It bubbled to the surface on the Kenai Peninsula. The first commercial wells in Alaska were drilled in 1901 by a British company. After World War I, the navy found a huge oil field near Point Barrow and set it aside for military use. In 1968, the oil companies

Oil refineries at Prudhoe Bay

discovered the largest oil field in the United States on state land at Prudhoe Bay. The state of Alaska auctioned off drilling rights, retaining a percentage of any oil found. Alaska collected $900 million in a few hours, and a new rush was on.

To get the oil to market, the oil companies decided to build a pipeline across Alaska to the ice-free port at Valdez, 800 miles (1,287 km) south. From there, supertankers would carry it to West Coast refineries. But those 800 miles crossed mountains, very environmentally sensitive land, and land whose ownership was in dispute between the federal government, state government, and Alaskan Natives.

About this time, the Middle East nations the supplied much of the oil to the United States raised prices and restricted sales to protest the United States's support of Israel. To clear the way for the pipeline, Congress quickly negotiated a settlement with the Federation of Alaskan Natives. It established thirteen regional corporations with eligible Natives as shareholders and gave the corporations the right to claim 44 million acres (17.8 million ha) of land and $962.5 million dollars. Most corporations have invested their share of the settlement money and land in arenas that provide jobs and income for members, including fishing, mining, hotels, financing business ventures, and scholarships.

Building a Pipeline

The Trans-Alaska Pipeline was the largest and most expensive private construction project in the world in 1974. It had two major problems: how to get oil, which comes out of the ground at 160°F (71°C), across permanently frozen land without melting it; and how

to keep the pipeline from cracking when it expands and contracts during weather changes or when it moves during earthquakes.

Welding pipe along the Trans-Alaska pipeline

    To solve these problems the designers raised portions of the superinsulated pipeline above the permafrost on special H-shaped supports. The supports release heat upward into the atmosphere, rather than into the ground. The pipeline also zigzags so it can con-

Pipeline Statistics

Cost $8 billion

Length and elevation 800 miles (1,287 km), from sea level at Prudhoe Bay to 4,800 feet (1,463 m) at Atiqun Pass and back to sea level at Valdez

Dimensions 4 feet (1.2 m) in diameter, 0.5 inch (1.25 cm) thick, wrapped in 4 inches (10 cm) of superinsulation.

Capacity Up to 84 million gallons (318 million l) of oil a day

Speed At 4 miles (6.4 km) per hour it takes 7.5 days for oil to travel the length of the pipeline

Buried One half of the pipeline is buried between 3 and 12 feet (1 and 4 m) deep. ∎

tract, expand, or move without cracking. In places, the pipeline is raised higher so migrating caribou can pass underneath.

It took more than 20,000 workers three years to build the pipeline. Wages were very high. People and money flowed into Alaska. Anchorage was the most expensive city in the United States. And it was the cheapest place to live in Alaska.

Finally, on June 20, 1977, the pipeline was ready. But that first drop of oil didn't arrive in Valdez until July 28, because of stops, checks, leaks, and accidents. Today, the oil travels the pipeline in about seven days, going through eleven pump stations that monitor it on its way to Valdez and to the cars and furnaces of America.

Exxon Valdez

On another Good Friday, the disaster the oil companies said would never happen happened. Since the pipeline began operating, nearly 9,000 safe trips had taken oil from Valdez through Prince William Sound. On the night of March 23, 1989, while heading through the sound, Captain Joseph Hazelwood of the *Exxon Valdez* shifted course to avoid icebergs. Then he told his third mate, Gregory Cousins, to take the helm and steer back on course in a few minutes. Captain Hazelwood went down to his cabin.

Cleanup operation at Valdez

Finding the Northwest Passage

From the discovery of the Americas, explorers searched for a water route through it. The last possibility seemed to be through the icy waters north of Alaska and Canada. But the ice free summers were too short. With help from Inuit, Roald Amundsen finally sailed through the Northwest Passage in a voyage that lasted from 1903 to 1906. It wasn't until 1969 that the first large ship, an icebreaker, made it through the passage in one year. ■

The supertanker is nearly 1,000 feet (305 m) long, about the length of three football fields, and can take as long as 3 miles (5 km) to stop. Although Cousins gave the orders to turn, the *Exxon Valdez* hit Bligh Reef. At 12:04 A.M., March 24, the rocks tore open the ship and 11 million gallons (42 million l) of crude oil poured out. The wind and current rapidly carried the oil southwest across the sound that is home to birds, fish, otters, whales, shore animals, and people.

The Alyeska Pipeline Service Company was not prepared to handle the largest oil spill in U.S. history. As they and the Exxon Company scrambled, the spill moved farther and farther along the shore, eventually covering 1,000 miles (1,609 km) of coastline, the distance from Cape Cod, Massachusetts, to Cape Hatteras, North Carolina.

Exxon hired fishers to skim oil from the water and workers to hose off the beaches and wipe off the rocks. Thousands of dead birds, otters, and fish washed ashore. Far more surely sank. The entire food chain and ecosystem of the sound was damaged. Winds, storms, and tides have cleaned up the mess further, and animal life is making a comeback. But the full extent of the ecological damage is not yet known.

Challenges for the Future

As Alaska looks to the future, it deals with issues that concern all states: creating a solid economic base, providing jobs and good schools for its citizens, controlling pollution, and dealing with social and health problems like alcoholism and domestic violence. But Alaska also has problems unique to it: the use and preservation of its resources and the appreciation and preservation of its Native cultures.

CHAPTER FIVE

Spectacular Nature

Alaska is so big, it covers several climatic and geographical regions. From the cold desert tundra in the Arctic, to the Ring of Fire volcanoes along the Aleutian Archipelago, to the temperate rain forest of the southeast, the parts of Alaska differ so much from one another, they are like different countries. Actually, Alaska is bigger than 200 of the world's countries. Alaska includes permafrost—permanently frozen ground—muskeg marshes, geothermal hot springs, glaciers, treeless tundra plains, fertile river valleys, boreal forests, mountains, alpine meadows, and even limestone caves.

Because Alaska and Hawaii are not part of the contiguous United States, which Alaskans call the Lower 48, the two states are often shown on maps in small boxes beside California. On such maps, Alaska may look like a small island but, superimposed over the United States, it stretches from the Atlantic to the Pacific, from Minnesota to Mexico. At 615,230 square miles (1.5 million sq km), Alaska equals 20 percent of the rest of the United States and is more than twice the size of Texas, the next-largest state.

Marshland in the Yukon-Kuskokwim Delta

Opposite: A view of the tundra in the Denali National Park

With one-third of the state above the Arctic Circle, Alaska is our northernmost state. It is also our westernmost, and because it crosses the 180° longitudinal line, it becomes our easternmost state. Although 500 miles (805 km) of Canada separate southeastern Alaska from Washington State, the 1,700-mile (2,736-km)-long Aleutian Island Chain dips so far south, it reaches a latitude just north of Seattle. Alaska lies so far west that Anchorage is north of Hawaii.

Regions of Alaska

The state of Alaska is divided into six regions separated by physical features and lifestyles: the Arctic, also called the North Slope; Western Alaska, along the Bering Sea coast; the Interior; Southcentral; Southeastern, also called the Panhandle; and the Alaska Peninsula and Aleutian Islands, also called the Chain. Anyplace out of the main population areas and off the road system is called the bush or rural Alaska.

Mountains

Many people think of mountains when they think of Alaska. And rightly so. Alaska has thirty-nine mountain ranges. Seventeen of the twenty-highest mountains in the United States are in Alaska. The highest is Mount McKinley, which Alaskans call Denali (Athabascan for "High One"). It's more than the highest mountain in North America; it's the longest above-sea-level slope in the world. It begins near sea level and rises to 20,320 feet (6,194 m). The taller mountains of the Himalayas are small peaks rising from a very high plateau.

Mount Megeik Volcano
in the Katmai National
Park

Alaska's Geographical Features

Total area; rank	615,230 sq. mi. (1,593,445 sq km); 1st
Land area; rank	570,374 sq. mi. (1,477,268 sq km); 1st
Water area; rank	44,856 sq. mi. (116,177 sq km); 1st
***Inland water;* rank**	17,501 sq. mi. (45,327 sq km); 1st
***Coastal water;* rank**	27,355 sq. mi. (70,849 sq km); 1st
Geographic center	60 miles (97 km) northwest of Mt. McKinley, 63° 50' N, 152° W
Highest point	Mount McKinley, 20,320 feet (6,194 m)
Lowest point	Sea level at the Pacific Ocean
Largest city	Anchorage
Longest river	The Yukon River flows 1,265 miles (2,036 km) within Alaska
Population; rank	626,932 (2000 census); 48th
Record high temperature	100°F (38°C) at Fort Yukon on June 27, 1915
Record low temperature	–80°F (–62°C) at Prospect Creek, near Stevens Village, on January 23, 1971
Average July temperature	55°F (13°C)
Average January temperature	5°F (–15°C)
Average annual precipitation	Varies from 5 inches (13 cm) in the Arctic to 300 inches (762 cm) along the southern coast

About eighty mountains in Alaska are active volcanoes. The Aleutian Islands are part of the Pacific Rim Ring of Fire, a chain of volcano peaks that circles the Pacific Ocean. There is almost always a steaming volcano on the Aleutian Chain, and larger eruptions every few years. Earthquakes are also common along the Ring of Fire.

Water

Alaska has more water than any state. Counting bays and islands, it has 33,904 miles (54,562 km) of saltwater tidelands, more than twice that of all the other states. There are more than 3 million lakes of 20 acres (8 ha) or larger. The largest, Iliamna Lake, at 1,150 square miles (2,976 sq km), is the second-largest freshwater lake wholly within the United States. Three thousand rivers and countless streams cross the state. The longest, the famed Yukon River,

The Alsek-Tatshenshinin River in the Tongass National Forest

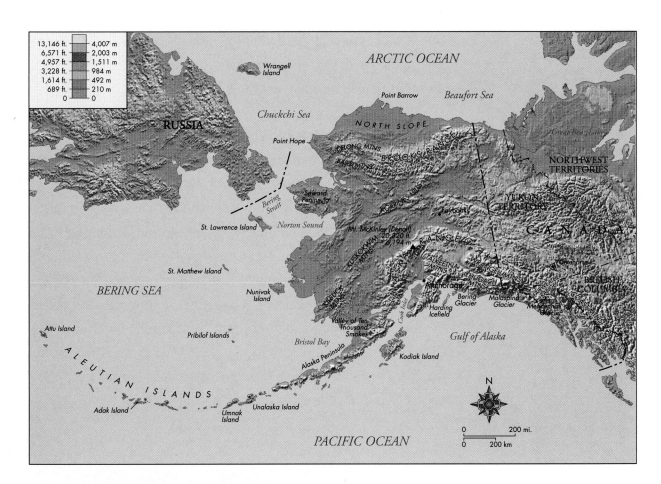

Alaska's topography

begins in Canada and flows 1,265 miles (2,036 km) through Alaska to the Bering Sea. It's the third-longest river in the United States, but has only one bridge. That is on the Dalton Highway, the road built to service the oil pipeline. An old miners' legend has it that if you spit into the Yukon River, you will one day return to Alaska.

Much of the water in Alaska is locked in ice. Its 100,000 glaciers contain three times more fresh water than all the lakes, rivers, and streams combined. Two ice fields, the Malaspina and the Bering, are each nearly twice as large as Rhode Island. Still,

Why Glaciers Look Blue

When light hits a glacier, the dense ice absorbs all colors of the visible light spectrum except the shortest waves. Those blue light waves bounce off the ice and are the only ones we can see. ■

glaciers only cover 4 percent of Alaska. Over the last several years, as the earth's atmosphere has warmed, many glaciers have been melting and rapidly receding.

Weather Alaskan Style

Alaska is so big that its climate is as varied as Minneapolis's climate is from Houston's. Because Alaska is bordered by ocean waters that hold warmth, its climate isn't as harsh as one might think. People from the Dakotas, Minnesota, and Michigan often claim they moved to Alaska for the warm winters. Schoolchildren usually have outside recess unless is it colder than –20°F (–29°C).

Mountainous Southeastern Alaska is a temperate rain forest with mild winters and cool summers. Some areas get 200 inches (508 cm) or more of precipitation a year. Winter rains frequently wash away snow at sea level, but the mountain slopes keep their deep snow and have terrific skiing.

The quiet village of Atka in the Aleutian Islands

Southcentral winters are usually pleasant, sunny, and warm at 10° to 30°F (–12° to –1°C). They rarely have more than a few weeks of –20° to –30°F (–29° to –34°C) weather. Thompson Pass, outside Valdez, receives the deepest snows in Alaska. In 1955, it recorded 62 inches (157 cm) in twenty-four hours. During the winter of 1952–53, the pass received nearly 1,000 feet (305 m) of snow. Summer highs range from about 60° to 70°F (16° to 21°C).

Warmed by the Japanese current, the Aleutian Islands have cool, cloudy, and windy summers and winters. Winters rarely have subzero temperatures but frequently have storms with 50-foot (15-m) seas and 100-mile per hour (161-kph) winds.

Interior Alaska, blocked by mountains from the warm ocean winds, gets the coldest temperatures in the winter, a record –80°F (–62°C), and the warmest in the summer, a record 100°F (38°C). It gets less rain and snow than the coastal areas, averaging only 13 inches (33 cm) a year.

In Western Alaska and the Arctic, summers are cool and winters are cold. In winter, winds blow in over the frozen ocean. In summer, the edges of the ice pack melt and it moves off shore, but the winds still blow cold. The north Arctic is a frozen desert averaging only 4 inches (10 cm) of precipitation a year. During the 1935–36 winter, just 3 inches (8 cm) of snow fell; 10 to 12 inches (25 to 30 cm) of snow melts to 1 inch (2.5 cm) of water.

Parklands

To some, Alaska seems like one huge beautiful park. This is understandable because more than half of all U.S. national park land is in Alaska. The government has set aside 300 million acres

A visitor at Glacier Bay

(121 million ha) of Alaska as preserves, monuments, wilderness areas, wildlife refuges, national forests, and national parks. Among the most visited parks are Denali, Glacier Bay, Katmai and the Valley of Ten Thousand Smokes, and the Kenai Fjords. Alaska also has the nation's largest state park system with 110 parks and 3.2 million acres (1.3 million ha).

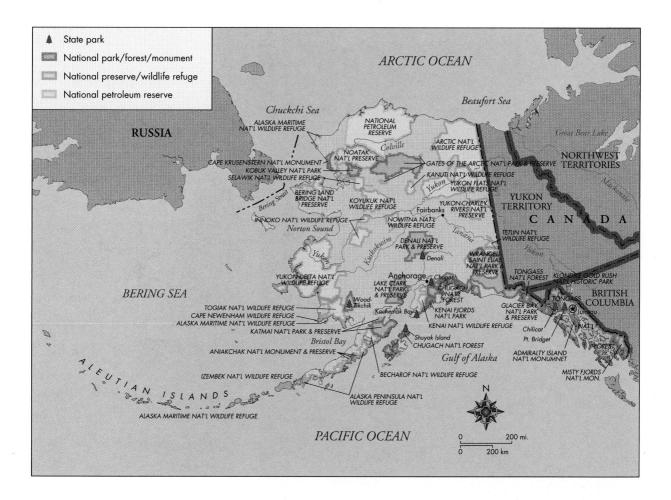

Alaska's parks and forests

Margaret Murie

Margaret Murie came to Fairbanks with her family in 1911 as a young girl. She grew up in the gold rush town and became the first woman to graduate from the University of Alaska. She married biologist Olaus Murie, and together they did some of the first scientific field research in Alaska. They both wrote books about their studies and experiences. Later she served on the governing council of the Wilderness Society. In the 1970s, she consulted with the federal government on the creation of the Gates of the Arctic National Park. In 1998, President Bill Clinton presented her with the Medal of Freedom for her environmental work. ■

The aurora borealis

Northern Lights

One of the really spectacular natural events in Alaska is the northern lights or aurora borealis. Storms on the sun send fragments of atoms streaming toward Earth. Some get caught by Earth's magnetic field and pulled toward the North and South Poles. Each time the atomic particles hit a particle of Earth's atmosphere, they glow, usually green, white, red, or purple. This appears as ribbons, bars, and waves of colored light flowing rapidly across the starry sky. Fairbanks is about the best place in the world to see this amazing sight, especially during September and April.

Alaskan Plants

Alaska has more than 1,500 species of plant life. Forests cover about a third of Alaska and tundra about half. Trees, bushes, and wildflowers grow on the tundra, but the cold and wind stunt their growth. Full-grown trees near Nome may be only 18 inches (46 cm) high and 0.5 inches (1.3 cm) in diameter. But Southeastern Sitka spruce near Juneau grow to more than 200 feet (61 cm) high and 6 feet (1.8m) in diameter. Other Alaskan trees are aspen, birch, cedar, hemlock, alder, and willow. Shrubs, grasses, wildflowers, and more than fifty kinds of berries grow thick in the forests or on the tundra.

In May, the tundra flowers all at once with sweeps of pink, purple, yellow, white, blue, and green. In the August autumn, the tundra turns vibrant red. A vast expanse of spruce, fir, and hemlock trees, the Southcentral and Interior's boreal forests shine gold in fall, turn red as the sap rises in late winter, and burst into green during one week in May. Southeastern's heavy forests are fragrant with fresh rain year-round. In the middle of winter, when most of Alaska is unrelentingly white, the Aleutian Islands' golden grassy slopes meet the green sea.

Fireweed grows prolifically on the tundra.

Alaska has hundreds of wilderness wildfires every summer. Most are started by lightning. They burn out the old decaying wood. The mineral-rich ash renews the soil for a healthier new forest that provides tender new plant growth for animals.

Alaskan Animals

Alaska has abundant wildlife, and few of its species are endangered. Its animals range from twenty-seven kinds of mosquitoes to the largest bears in the world. Alaska has three types of bear. Polar bears, really marine mammals, live along the Arctic Ocean. They have been seen swimming 50 miles (80 km) from land or ice. Brown, or grizzly, bears live from Southeastern to the Arctic Circle.

A grizzly bear fishing

Those on Kodiak Island, known as Kodiak bears, grow to 12 feet (3.7 m) high and weigh more than 1,000 pounds (454 kg). Black bears live in forests all over the state.

Other animals in Alaska are moose, caribou, musk oxen, wolves, mountain goats, and Dall sheep. Alaska also has coyotes, deer, elk, and even a herd of buffalo transplanted from Montana eighty years ago. Among its smaller mammals are foxes, lynx, minks, ermines, marmots, muskrats, beavers, rabbits, lemmings, porcupines, and a whole variety of rodents.

Alaska's oceans and seas teem with marine animals, including sea otters, sea lions, seals, walrus, dolphins, porpoise, and twenty species of whales. Because of overhunting, all marine mammals are

Visitors come to Alaska to see humpback whales.

The Life of a Salmon

Salmon hatch from eggs laid in freshwater streams, and, when only a few inches long, swim downstream to the ocean. After three to five years, the adults swim back to the exact spot in the exact stream where they hatched. When they reach fresh water, they begin to turn red. Rivers become so thick with salmon, they look like red tiled walkways. All along the journey, predators feed on the millions of migrating salmon—whales, seals, bears, eagles, and people. Those salmon that make it back to their birthplace lay thousands of eggs apiece and then die. From all those eggs, only two or three salmon make it all the way back to reproduce. ■

now protected. Only Alaskan Natives with an ancestral history and subsistence lifestyle are allowed to hunt them.

Alaska has the most generously abundant fisheries in the world: halibut that can weigh well over 300 pounds (136 kg), five varieties of salmon, herring, rockfish, pollock, cod, snapper, shrimp, oysters, mussels, and crab. Some king crab measure 7 feet (2 m) from claw to claw.

About 20 million birds migrate to Alaska from around the world to breed in the lush summers. Scientists have counted more

Swans in flight over the tundra

Denali—The High One

Alaska's most visited national park is Denali, home to Mount McKinley, the highest mountain in North America (left). In 1896, a prospector from Ohio, William Dickey, left Alaska. The first news he heard after leaving the bush was that William McKinley, also from Ohio, was nominated for the presidency. He named the mountain he loved after McKinley and worked to make it official. At that time, the mountain already had the Native name *Denali*, the "high one." Alaska officially calls the mountain Denali, but it remains Mount McKinley on national maps.

The 6-million-acre (2.4-million-ha) park and preserve is bigger than Massachusetts. At the park entrance are exhibits, ranger talks, dogsled demonstrations, and hiking trails. Although visitors may backpack into the wilderness, most take a one-day bus tour. They usually see caribou, grizzly bears, and Dall sheep and often see foxes, wolves, moose, marmots, eagles, and other birds.

The park road begins in the forest but quickly winds upward to the alpine tundra. It crosses milky glacier-fed rivers and passes the grassy hillsides where grizzlies roam and the rocky mountainsides are dotted with Dall sheep. The

than 200,000 birds flying by in a single hour in the Copper River Delta. Of Alaska's 443 different species of birds, only about 200 species stay year-round. Rufus hummingbirds fly 2,000 miles (3,219 km) from Mexico to southeastern Alaska. Swans fly in from as far away as North Carolina. Arctic terns come from Antarctica, 20,000 miles (32,187 km) away. Siberian snow geese winter on Alaska's southcentral coast and Canadian snow geese summer in the Arctic wildlife refuge. Bald eagles, 3,500 strong, migrate

road continues past Polychrome Ridge, a horizon of red, rust, orange, yellow, and purple cliffs and on to Eielson Visitors Center. This is the best place to view Denali, although the mountain is often buried in clouds. Caribou graze around the center. Inside, seismic equipment records earthquakes.

If you continue down the road, past the glacier walls, you come to Wonder Lake (above). The wonder is the quiet beauty of the Denali backcountry, the reflection of the great mountain in the smooth lake, fireweed blooming, moose wading in the marshy water, loons calling. This is land as the ancients knew it 20,000 years ago. ■

from inland Alaska to feed on a winter run of salmon near Haines. Alaska has more bald eagles than all the rest of the United States combined.

While Alaska may have more of many things, Alaska has no snakes, or reptiles of any kind. It's just too cold.

CHAPTER SIX

Cities, Towns, and Villages

The Dalton Highway
along the Brooks
Range

Life is very different in Alaska's large cities than in its bush communities. Cities, such as Anchorage, Fairbanks, and Juneau, are population and economic centers for the state. Towns, such as Barrow, Nome, Bethel, and Ketchikan, offer regional support to nearby villages. Villages are small, and much of their population may be Natives keeping many of the traditions of their ancestors. No matter where people live in Alaska, they enjoy great scenery, being close to nature, and outdoor activities.

Off the Road

Some of Alaska's most interesting towns are those most difficult to visit. Alaska still has few roads connecting towns. This has helped many rural villages maintain their traditional ways; however, television has reached where roads have not. Although sixty times larger, Alaska has about as many miles of road as Vermont. But only half of Alaska's are paved. Flying is the most common way to

Opposite:
The Chugach
Mountains in
Anchorage

get around the state. Most villages have airstrips, even if they don't have cars. People in the bush use snowmobiles, all-terrain vehicles, boats, dogsleds, and their legs!

New roads have been proposed, and some will likely be built. However, not everyone is happy about that because once villages are tied to the road system, the character of their communities changes.

Barrow, the Largest Inupiat Village

The northernmost town in the United States, and one of the most unique, is Barrow. Barrow is on the Arctic Ocean 1,300 miles (2,092 km) from the North Pole. In winter, the sun sets and doesn't come above the horizon for sixty-nine days. But eighty-four days of summer go by without the sun ever dipping below the horizon. Barrow has a population of 4,581 and, although it

Caribou skins drying

now has many ethnic groups, it is still essentially an Inupiat village. Barrow has city things many villages don't, like indoor plumbing, modern designed buildings, big schools, and a hospital. In the grocery store, you can buy fresh fruit from Hawaii, lettuce from Mexico, or milk and eggs from Washington. But Barrow has maintained its Inupiat roots. In the late summer, as animals begin their migration south, it is a hunting and fishing town. Caribou skins are stretched and tanned in front yards, smoked seal meat, fish, and birds hang on drying racks while whaling crews watch for spouts on the ocean. On the beach, strips of whale baleen weather, waiting for winter and Native craftspeople.

Since fur trading days, when molasses and yeast were added to a Native tea of bark and berries creating alcoholic *hoochenoo*, alcohol has been a danger to the health of Native communities. Barrow, like many communities, restricts alcohol use. The restrictions have helped control some problems.

But Barrow has other problems uncommon to most United States cities. A few years ago, Halloween was nearly canceled because so many polar bears were wandering into town. With the help of adult guards, goblins filled the streets and their candy bags.

Tourists have discovered Barrow. During the summer, plane loads land each day. Dancers perform while elders tell stories and teach about the Native ways. Artists sell their carvings, skin boots, masks, and dolls to visitors so that they may take home memories of another life and time that has been preserved on the far north ocean of the United States.

How Nome Got Its Name

Nome's name was all a mistake. Prospectors called this settlement Anvil City. The natives called the area *Ayasayuk*, "sheer cliff," and the Russians named it *Mys Tolstoi*, "broad cape." A British navy cartographer creating maps from ships' charts misread the handwriting that said "?name" to mean "Nome." ■

Nome, on the Edge of the Land Bridge

In 1899, Nome was the largest city in Alaska, with more than 20,000 miners camped on the beaches panning for gold. Now 3,505 people live in Nome. Mining, tourism, and, for Natives, reindeer herding, provide income. Nome is laid out along the Norton Sound shore with straight rows of buildings spreading back into the flat plains. It is accessible only by boat and plane.

Cape Nome is the remains of the Bering Land Bridge where people first crossed into the Western Hemisphere. The Bering Land Bridge National Preserve near town has been set aside to remain as it was when the first Asians crossing into the new continent saw it.

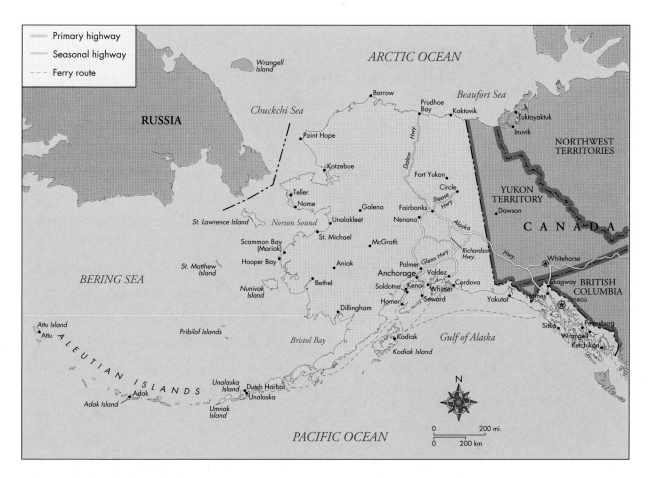

The map shows the following labels:

Legend:
— Primary highway
— Seasonal highway
-- Ferry route

ARCTIC OCEAN

Wrangell Island

Chuckchi Sea

RUSSIA

Barrow
Prudhoe Bay
Kaktovik
Beaufort Sea
Tuktoyaktuk
Inuvik

NORTHWEST TERRITORIES

Point Hope
Dalton Hwy.
Fort Yukon
Circle
Kotzebue
Steese Hwy.
YUKON TERRITORY
Dawson
Teller
Nome
Fairbanks
CANADA
Galena
Nenana
Alaska Hwy.
St. Lawrence Island
Norton Sound
Unalakleet
Whitehorse
Scammon Bay (Mariak)
St. Michael
McGrath
Richardson Hwy.
Hooper Bay
Glenn Hwy.
Palmer
Hwy.
Skagway
BRITISH COLUMBIA
St. Matthew Island
Aniak
Anchorage
Valdez
Haines
Juneau
Bethel
Soldotna Kenai
Whittier
Cordova
BERING SEA
Nunivak Island
Homer
Seward
Yakutat
Dillingham
Sitka
Petersburg
Wrangell
Ketchikan
Attu Island
Attu
Pribilof Islands
Bristol Bay
Kodiak
Gulf of Alaska
ALEUTIAN ISLANDS
Kodiak Island
Adak
Adak Island
Unalaska Island
Dutch Harbor
Unalaska
Umnak Island

PACIFIC OCEAN

N

0   200 mi.
0   200 km

The sea is still Nome's encroaching enemy, and the Army Corps of Engineers has built a retaining seawall to keep winter storms from washing the beach and town away. Golfers play on a course laid out on the frozen Bering Sea with Astroturf greens using brightly colored balls on the white fairways.

Nome is well known for gold and dogs. In summer, people still come to mine the beaches. In winter, people flock to Nome for the finish of the famed Iditarod Trail Sled Dog Race. Nome should be known for its sunsets. It has some of the most beautiful sunsets in the world. Brilliant waves of gold, scarlet, and fuchsia wash over the Bering Sea and reflect in every window, on every wall.

Alaska's cities and highways

Opposite: Winter in Nome

Fairbanks, the Center of the State

Near the center of the state, Fairbanks is a bustling city of 30,224 people. It was born in the gold rush and named for the best friend of respected Judge James Wickersham, Indiana senator Charles Fairbanks. It is nestled in the valley where the Chena River joins the Tanana and is surround by forested hills. Tourism, oil, coal, gold mining, education, Arctic research, and the military are major employers.

For Alaska, Fairbanks is an old town. It had electricity, sewers, police, a fire department, hospital, library, and school system by 1908. It got a university in 1917. Yet Fairbanks has the energy of a frontier town. Things always seem to be happening in Fairbanks. An average January day reaches –2°F (–19°C), perfect for dog sledding and playing hockey. In July, the days average 72°F (22°C) and

The Chena River winds through Fairbanks as the Tanana flows in the distance.

the city floods with tourists. Some take stern-wheeler rides to an Athabascan fish camp or go river rafting. Others tee off for a golf game at midnight or visit the nearby Trans-Alaska Oil Pipeline.

Anchorage and the Road South

Anchorage is Alaska's largest city, with 260,283 people, nearly half the state's population. It is the economic center of the state. Anchorage appears much like any other town in America: nice houses, apartments, malls, and tall downtown buildings. It has excellent restaurants, theaters, opera, museums, and rush hour traffic jams. In winter, the entire town decorates with white lights; in summer, brilliant flowers abound in all public places and most private homes.

However, Anchorage is still very close to its wilderness roots. Moose graze in backyard gardens, bald eagles sit on streetlights, grizzly bears follow the salmon streams into downtown, mountain goats come down onto the Seward Highway, and hundreds of Canada geese nest on the library lawn.

Anchorage lies on Cook Inlet and is fenced by the Chugach Mountains. In town are Kincaid and Bicentennial

Downtown Anchorage

Blue Babe

In the dead of winter 36,000 years ago, two Pleistocene Alaskan lions attacked and killed a steppe bison. For three days, they nibbled on it. But the bison froze so hard that one of the lions broke a tooth and they abandoned it. Thirty-six thousand years later, gold miners excavating a permafrost hillside outside of Fairbanks washed away gravel to see a large lump that they thought looked like a boulder. But it was the lions' kill. Blue Babe, the perfectly preserved steppe bison mummy, is one of only three complete steppe bison in the world. Today, Blue Babe, with claw marks and tooth holes visible in its hide, is on display at the University of Alaska Museum in Fairbanks. ∎

The Alyeska Resort in Girdwood, located in Southcentral Alaska

Parks. These large natural areas have a ski area and trails for sled dogs, cross-country skiing, biking, running, and horseback riding. Several lakes in Anchorage are stocked with trout, and most of the creeks have salmon runs.

The Seward Highway heads south of town with cliffs on one side and Turnagain Arm and mountains on the other. Occasionally, a bore tide, a 3-foot (1-m) wall of water, rushes into the fjord. This area has some of the world's fastest tides. Strong winds make Turnagain Arm a great place for wind surfing, but wet suits are a must. People rock- and ice-climb the cliffs, near where mountain goats walk. There are world-class skiing and snowboarding at Alyeska Resort farther down the highway, and several glaciers lie just beyond that. In the fall, whales follow herring and salmon runs into Turnagain Arm.

At one end of the Y-shaped road heading south from Anchorage is Seward. As in most seaside towns in southern Alaska, fishing, shrimping, and crabbing are major occupations and recreations. Seward has the world's largest silver salmon derby, the Alaska Sealife Center aquarium, and a Fourth of July celebration that draws thousands of people. Many come to run or watch the Mount Marathon footrace which goes straight up and back down a mountain.

A Mount Marathon Race runner in Seward

The other branch of the road leads to Homer on Kachemak Bay. Homer is built against the mountain bluffs on the edge of the bright blue bay surrounded by white topped mountains. The beauty of Homer has drawn many artists and writers to move there. Nearby is a community of Old Believers, a group of Russian immigrants who came to Alaska looking for religious freedom.

Dutch Harbor and Unalaska

The small twin towns of Dutch Harbor and Unalaska, together with about 4,300 people, lie on deep, well-protected harbors on the ice-free Aleutian Chain. Dutch Harbor is one of the busiest fishing ports in the United States. Fishing fleets from around the world

The Alaska Zoo

The zoo in Anchorage features mostly northern animals such as musk ox, bear, moose, and Siberian tigers. Sammy Seawell started it after appearing on a television game show and winning a baby elephant. She was thrilled and refused the $3,000 substitution prize. No one had ever done that, and the show didn't even know where to get an elephant. But they did. For many years, Annabelle the elephant was the delight of Anchorage children. Although they were used to seeing moose in their backyards, many had never seen an elephant. Once Annabelle even flew to Nome just so the children there could see an elephant. ■

dock, ship fish, and refuel there. Walking down the street, you might hear ten different languages. Across the bridge, officially named Bridge to the Other Side, lies Unalaska, centered around the historic cathedral, the Holy Ascension of Christ, one of many Russian Orthodox churches found on the Aleutian Chain.

Juneau and Down the Panhandle

Juneau, built on Gastineau Channel against the steep mountainside, is the only state capital inaccessible by road. You must take a boat

Camping out above the Mendenhall Glacier

Juneau's Beginnings

In 1880, Chief Kowee of the Auk Tribe took ore samples from Quartz Gulch to George Pilz, a Sitka merchant who had offered rewards and jobs for promising gold leads. Pilz grubstaked Joseph Juneau and Richard Harris to look for gold. In spite of being more interested in drinking than prospecting, under Chief Kowee's guidance, they made the first major gold strike in Alaska. Miners poured into the Juneau area, and eventually more than $158 million worth of gold was taken from the area's mines. Neither Juneau nor Harris held on to their money for long. But both left their names on the settlement that grew where they found gold. Finally, a vote decided that Juneau, not Harrisburg, would be the town's name, probably because Juneau paid more for his votes than Harris did. ■

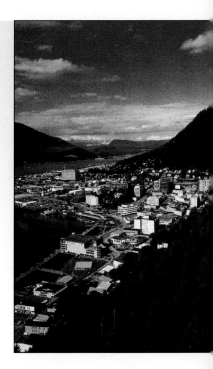

or plane to Juneau. It often rains in Juneau, but on those rare sunny days, this town of 30,711 shines like a blue and green jewel. The beauty of Juneau makes it a favorite stop for cruise ships. In summer, several ships a day dock there. Thousands of passengers stream into town climbing the steep hills to souvenir shops, museums, and to visit Mendenhall Glacier.

In January, when the tourists are long gone, Juneau's second invasion begins. Legislators and their staffs come from all over the state for the congressional session. Fishing, mining, tourism, and government work provide most of the jobs in the area. Hiking, skiing, fishing, kayaking, and boating provide much of the fun.

In Sitka, people can still see Russian America as they walk the streets. Stroll past St. Michael's Cathedral, the bishop's house, the old blockhouse, the Russian cemetery, and Princess Maksoutov's grave. Drink Russian tea from a samovar. Eat Russian tea cakes.

Lincoln in Alaska

In 1869, when Secretary of State William Henry Seward visited Alaska, the Tlingit Raven tribe was impressed with news of President Abraham Lincoln's work to end slavery. They carved a red cedar totem pole in his honor with a Raven as the base and Lincoln on the top. This was fifty years before the Lincoln Memorial in Washington D.C. Over the years, the totem pole was battered by weather and a spruce tree began growing in Lincoln's pocket. Today, the top of the Lincoln pole is in the State Museum in Juneau. In 1940, two new poles were carved, one for Saxman Village and the other for Springfield, Illinois. ■

Watch the New Archangel dancers in their Russian costumes. Overlooking the town is Castle Hill, the site of Lord Baranof's Castle, where Alaska was turned over to the United States. In 1894, the Russian governor's house burned; however, the old Russian cannons still point out to sea as they did centuries ago.

There is more to Sitka than history, though. Sitka has a beautiful harbor, mountains, forests, muskeg marshes, a summer music festival, Native heritage, totem poles, and the Alaska Raptor Rehabilitation Center. There injured birds of prey such as eagles and falcons are nursed back to health and released into the wild when possible.

At the south end of the panhandle is Ketchikan. The town that has bounced from gold boom to cannery boom to timber boom now lives on tourism and fishing. Much of Ketchikan is built on pilings and along wooden walkways over the water. Boats line the docks in front of the town. Ketchikan is well known for its totem poles carved from huge cedar trees. More totem poles are found here at

An eagle totem in Ketchikan

the Totem Heritage Center, Totem Bight State Historical Park, and the nearby village of Saxman than anywhere else in the world. A totem pole often tells the story of a family or clan's history and honors their important people or events.

CHAPTER SEVEN

Government by the People

Although Alaska is the largest state, it is one of the least populated. This makes it possible for most people to know personally their government officials. With so few people, every vote, every opinion, counts. Often, elections are decided by only a few votes.

Four forms of government affect Alaska: the federal government, the state government, area governments called boroughs, and city councils. In many towns, the Native corporations also have a great deal of influence.

Alaska's state courthouse and capitol

Like the federal government, the state of Alaska has three branches: the executive, or governor's office; the legislative, which is divided into a twenty-member senate and a forty-member house of representatives; and the judicial. There are fifteen state departments headed by commissioners, most appointed by the governor.

The governor and lieutenant governor serve together. They are elected for four years and may serve two consecutive terms. Senators are also elected for four years and representatives for two. Both may run as many times as they like. Every ten years, after the census, election districts can be redrawn to keep an equal number of people in each district. A constitutional amendment limits the

Opposite: Fourth of July parade in downtown Juneau

Alaska's Governors

Name	Party	Term	Name	Party	Term
William A. Egan	Dem.	1959–1966	Bill Sheffield	Dem.	1982–1986
Walter J. Hickel	Rep.	1966–1969	Steve Cowper	Dem.	1986–1990
Keith Miller	Rep.	1969–1970	Walter J. Hickel	Ind.	1990–1994
William A. Egan	Dem.	1970–1974	Tony Knowles	Dem.	1994–2002
Jay S. Hammond	Rep.	1974–1982	Frank Murkowski	Rep.	2002–

legislative session to 120 days. Like all states, Alaska has two U.S. senators, but because of its small population, only one congressperson.

About 44 percent of Alaska is divided into sixteen boroughs, much like county governments. The rest of the land is sparsely populated or under federal control. Within a borough, there can be several city governments. Some area governments, such as the Municipality of Anchorage, function as both borough and city. Most local elections are nonpartisan, which means that the candidates don't represent political parties. Among the locally elected nonpartisan positions are city or borough mayors and council or assembly members.

The State Constitution

To prepare for statehood, Alaska decided to follow the plan Tennessee used to gain statehood, and create a constitution first. In 1955, Alaska held a constitutional convention at the University in Fairbanks, in what has been renamed Constitution Hall. Fortunately, Alaska had forty-eight other state constitutions to review. The fifty-five delegates from around the state crafted a very short

The state capitol in Juneau

(14,000-word) document setting up the structure and procedures for the future state. The document favors a strong governor. The National Municipal League called it "one of the best, if not the best state constitution ever written." The voters approved the constitu-

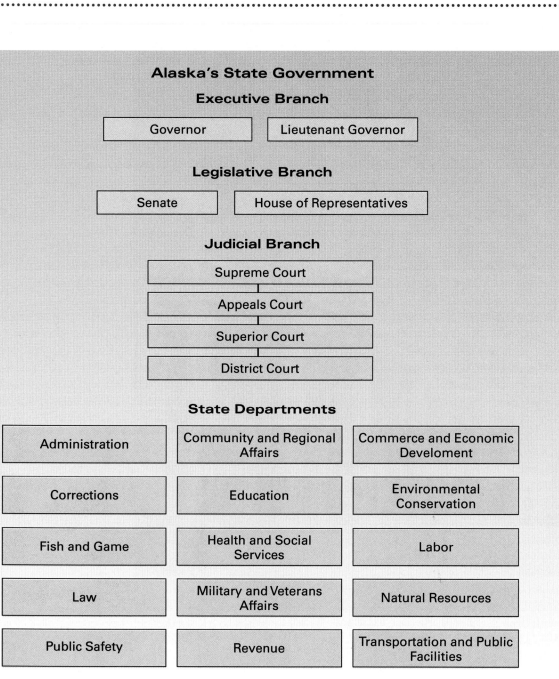

Alaska's State Government

Executive Branch

| Governor | Lieutenant Governor |

Legislative Branch

| Senate | House of Representatives |

Judicial Branch

Supreme Court

Appeals Court

Superior Court

District Court

State Departments

Administration	Community and Regional Affairs	Commerce and Economic Develoment
Corrections	Education	Environmental Conservation
Fish and Game	Health and Social Services	Labor
Law	Military and Veterans Affairs	Natural Resources
Public Safety	Revenue	Transportation and Public Facilities

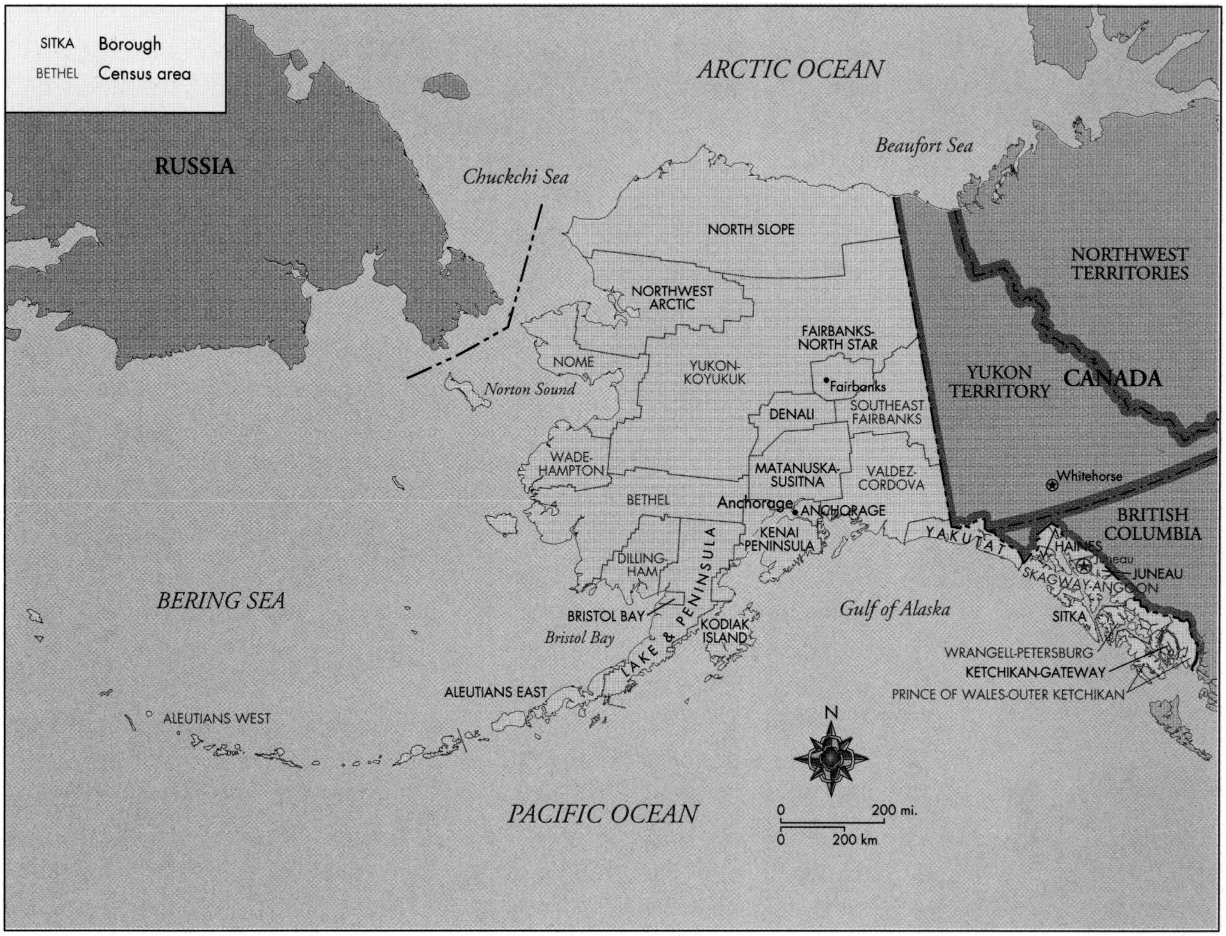
SITKA Borough
BETHEL Census area
ARCTIC OCEAN
RUSSIA
Chuckchi Sea
Beaufort Sea
NORTH SLOPE
NORTHWEST ARCTIC
NORTHWEST TERRITORIES
FAIRBANKS-NORTH STAR
NOME
Norton Sound
YUKON-KOYUKUK
Fairbanks
SOUTHEAST FAIRBANKS
DENALI
YUKON TERRITORY
CANADA
WADE-HAMPTON
MATANUSKA-SUSITNA
VALDEZ-CORDOVA
Whitehorse
BETHEL
Anchorage
ANCHORAGE
KENAI PENINSULA
BRITISH COLUMBIA
YAKUTAT
HAINES
Juneau
JUNEAU
DILLING-HAM
LAKE & PENINSULA
SKAGWAY-ANGOON
BERING SEA
Gulf of Alaska
BRISTOL BAY
Bristol Bay
KODIAK ISLAND
SITKA
WRANGELL-PETERSBURG
KETCHIKAN-GATEWAY
ALEUTIANS EAST
PRINCE OF WALES-OUTER KETCHIKAN
ALEUTIANS WEST
N
PACIFIC OCEAN
0 200 mi.
0 200 km

Alaska's boroughs

tion in 1956 and awaited statehood which came on January 3, 1959. Since statehood, new issues have caused the constitution to be amended several times. Currently, the state is wrestling with the issue of access to and preservation of its natural resources, especially fish and game. Historical use, economic development, and recreational use sometimes conflict, and the legislature is attempting to prioritize the use of natural resources.

Political Leaders

Tony Knowles

Tony Knowles (left), a native Okla-homan, was elected Alaska's ninth governor in 1994. He came to Alaska to work in the oil fields after serving in Vietnam and graduating from Yale University. He liked Alaska so much, he stayed and entered the restaurant business. He still owns the Downtown Deli in Anchorage, which specializes in reindeer stew.

Knowles served in the Anchor-age Assembly before being elected mayor. As mayor, he supervised construction of a new water sys-tem, landfill, many public buildings, roads, and parks. An avid runner, one of Knowles' favorite projects was a bike and jogging trail along Turnagain Arm. To honor him, the Anchorage Assembly named it the Tony Knowles Trail.

His focus as governor was fiscal responsibility, economic develop-ment, education, children's issues, and environmental protection. Knowles has said that business and government are similar: "You give the customers what they want; you always live within your means; and you roll up your sleeves to do whatever needs to be done." In between public-service jobs, he is often found practicing what he preaches, helping to bus tables and serve customers at his restaurant.

Fran Ulmer

Fran Ulmer received degrees in economics, political science, and law from the University of Wiscon-sin in her home state. Then she and her family moved to Alaska, where she immediately became involved in politics. She served as Juneau's mayor and several terms in the House of Representatives. There she promoted justice, edu-cation, children's issues, and envi-ronmental legislation. In 1994, Ulmer was elected Alaska's first woman lieutenant governor.

Jay S. Hammond

Jay S. Hammond (below left) likes to call himself the "bush rat" gov-ernor. Hammond grew up in New York and Vermont. He served as a fighter pilot during World War II. After being stationed in Alaska dur-ing the war, he decided to make the state his home. He earned a degree in biology at the University of Alaska and homesteaded at Lake Clark. Over the years he worked as a fisher, hunter, trapper, wildlife guide, and for the U.S. Fish and Wildlife Service. In 1958, he was elected to the state house of representatives and later to the state senate. In 1974, he was elected governor. He oversaw the state during the chaotic years of building the pipeline and was instrumental in establishing the Permanent Fund for Alaskans. Today, he lives at his Lake Clark homestead and writes books of humor and memoirs.

William L. Hensley

William L. Hensley (below right), an Inupiat, was born in Kotzebue. He and his family lived in traditional sod houses, and as a child, he helped his family fish and hunt for food. He eagerly attended school whenever he could. Because there were no high schools in the region, a missionary arranged for him to attend boarding school in Tennessee. He graduated from George Washington University in Washington, D.C., majoring in political science, and later attended the University of Alaska for graduate studies.

As a boy, Hensley watched the federal government auction off traditional Native land for homesites in Kotzebue. While in college, Hensley studied the issue of Native land claims. In graduate school, he wrote a landmark paper, "What Rights to Land Have the Alaska Natives?" He helped to form the Alaska Federation of Natives (AFN) in 1966 and to file a claim with the federal government for Natives' traditional lands. The claim was settled by conveying to the Alaskan Native corporations official title to 44 million acres (18 million ha) of land and nearly $1 billion.

Hensley has served in the state house of representatives, state senate, and on several state and national government committees. He has held many positions within the Native community, including president of the AFN. In business, he has served as chairman of a bank and as an executive of the Alyeska Pipeline Service Company. He continues to work on education, health, the arts, the environment, Native concerns, and on the general well-being of the state of Alaska. ■

Alaska's State Symbols

State bird: Willow ptarmigan Adopted in 1955, this 15-inch (38-cm) Arctic grouse is brown in summer and white in winter and lives in woods and tundra throughout Alaska.

Marine mammal: Bowhead whale Adopted in 1983, the bowhead migrates to Alaska's waters to feed in the summers.

Land mammal: Moose Adopted in 1998, the moose, the largest member of the deer family, may weigh as much as 1,500 pounds (680 kg). Moose live in the forest of mainland Alaska and often enter towns looking for food.

Fish: King or Chinook salmon Adopted in 1962, these monster fish provide some of the state's best sports fishing. Twenty-pounders are frequently thrown back for being too small. The record fish is 97 pounds 4 ounces (44 kg) and was caught on the Kenai River in 1985.

Fossil: Woolly mammoth Adopted in 1986, the fossils and tusks of woolly mammoths are found mostly in Interior Alaska.

Flower: Forget-me-not Adopted in 1949, this delicate looking small blue flower is hardy enough to grow wild across the entire state.

Tree: Sitka spruce Adopted in 1962, this huge tree can grow to more than 200 feet (61 m) tall and more than 6 feet (1.8 m) in diameter. It grows mainly in Southeastern Alaska.

Gem: Jade Adopted in 1968, Alaska has much high-quality jade. Most is in the northwest. Kobuk Mountain, near Kotzebue, is almost entirely jade.

Mineral: Gold Adopted in 1968, gold was the catalyst for growth in the far north, although Alaska has valuable minerals more abundant than gold.

Sport: Dog sled racing (mushing) Adopted in 1972, this sport is born out of the main form of transportation of early Alaska. Mushers use specially bred dogs who love to run more than anything. ∎

Alaska's State Flag

In 1926, the Alaskan Territory decided to hold a contest for 7th to 12th grade students to design an official flag. The selection committee was captivated by the simplicity, elegance, and appropriateness of thirteen-year-old Benny Benson's design. He won a $1,000 scholarship and a watch. His design, the golden Big Dipper and North Star on a dark blue background, was accompanied by Benson's words:

"The blue field is for the Alaska sky and the forget-me-not, an Alaskan flower. The North Star is for the future state of Alaska, the most northerly of the Union. The dipper is for the Great Bear—symbolizing strength."

Benny Benson was a young Native living at the mission school in Seward when he created his award-winning design. People liked it so much, the Constitutional Convention voted to have it remain as the state flag. Although Benson studied engineering, he followed his dream of becoming a commercial fisher. Throughout his life, everyone respected him for his kindness and gentle nature. He died in 1972. Today, one of the main streets of Anchorage is named Benson Boulevard in honor of Benny. ■

Alaska's State Song
"Alaska's Flag"

In 1935, Marie Drake, who worked for the Commissioner of Education, wrote a poem about Benny's flag for the cover of the *School Bulletin* newsletter. Later, Elinor Dusenbury set Drake's words to music, and in 1955, the song became the official territorial and then state song.

Eight stars of gold on a field of blue,
Alaska's Flag, may it mean to you
The blue of the sea, the evening sky,
The mountain lakes and the flow'rs nearby,
The gold of the early sourdough dreams,
The precious gold of the hills and streams,

The brilliant stars in the northern sky,
The Bear, the Dipper, and shining high,
The great North star with its steady light.
O'er land and sea a beacon bright,
Alaska's Flag to Alaskans dear,
The simple flag of a last frontier.

CHAPTER EIGHT

Making a Living

The economy of Alaska swings up and down with the latest boom and bust. These days it is swinging with the price of oil. Alaska produces 25 percent of all the nation's oil. Much of that oil comes from state-owned land. Alaska gets a percentage of every barrel sold. Oil and natural gas provide Alaska with 90 percent of its state income and 20 percent of its jobs. Alaskans have no state income tax and no state sales tax. Oil pays almost all the bills. However, as the price of oil falls, and the North Slope reserves dwindle, Alaska is trying to develop other more stable sources of revenue.

Fishing for crabs

Alaska's Natural Resources

Alaska is a resource production state from its fisheries to its forests to its minerals—oil, natural gas, coal, zinc, gold, copper, and many more. There is little heavy industry beyond resource production.

People around the world enjoy Alaskan wild salmon, halibut, crab, shrimp, herring, and fish roe (eggs used as caviar). Today, Alaska's fishery catch of nearly 6 billion pounds (2.7 billion kg) is about four times greater than Louisiana's, the state with the next-largest catch. However, until 1976 the fishing industry had been declining dramatically. Foreign fishing fleets were overfishing just off Alaskan shores. To solve this problem, the 1976 Magneson Act extended the United States' control of fishing in its ocean waters

Opposite: The Tesoro Oil Refinery on the Kenai Peninsula

from 3 miles (5 km) to 200 miles (322 km). Now salmon have returned in record numbers, and the almost-depleted king crab harvest is healthy again.

Mining continues to play a strong role in Alaska's economy. Nowhere in North America is there as much mining potential as in Alaska. In addition to large stores of zinc, there are major stores of coal, natural gas, and oil. The North Slope has even more natural gas than oil, and developers hope to build a natural gas pipeline next to the oil pipeline.

Today, one of Alaska's most valuable resources is its wild landscape. Alaska's great vistas make it a favorite backdrop for television, film, commercials, and photography. In growing numbers

Alaska's natural resources

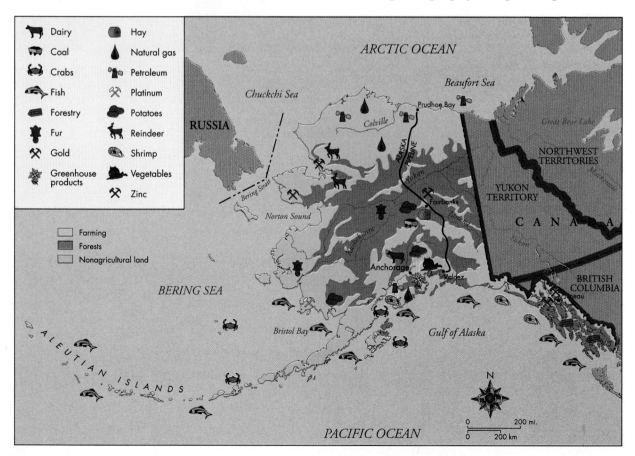

each year, Alaska draws millions of tourists eager to see Alaska's splendor and abundant wildlife. Ecotourism may be the state's next big economic boom.

Making a Living

The high prices and wages during the building of the pipeline have moderated. At that time, Alaska's cost of living was the highest in the nation. Now Anchorage's is similar to Seattle's or Washington, D.C.'s, but costs still remain very high in the villages. Fortunately, Alaskans' wages are among the nation's highest.

A salmon bake

Alaskans' major employers are the government (military, federal, and state), fishing, mining, trade, transportation, and service-oriented businesses.

Although Alaska supports major industries like oil and fisheries, the state encourages and promotes individual inventiveness. Many people have created thriving small businesses associated with Alaska, such as bottling glacier water, manufacturing airplane floats, and making gourmet wild berry chocolates. Salmon is processed into many specialty foods and products, such as salmon nuggets, salmon dog treats, and salmon skin wallets. Reindeer sausage is popular with residents and tourists, and powdered reindeer antler is sent to Asia for use in medicines.

The booming tourist industry has pro-

A logging dock master in Hobart Bay

vided many new opportunities, such as making souvenirs. *Ulus*, a tourist favorite, are circular knives with wooden, stone, jade, or bone handles based on a Native seal skinning knife design. Many Native village women knit *qiviut*, the soft underhair of the musk oxen, more luxurious than cashmere, into beautiful scarves, hats, and stoles. These special designs, reflective of the knitter's village, are sold in stores in Alaska and other major cities. Tourism also offers many opportunities ranging from guide services to wildlife-viewing tours to bed-and-breakfasts.

Economic opportunities are harder to come by in rural Alaska, where only 40 percent of the people may have a regular job. A subsistence lifestyle consisting of hunting, fishing, and Native craftwork remains important. There is seasonal work in construction, fisheries, forestry, and fire fighting.

One important source of revenue, especially in rural Alaska, is the Alaska Permanent Fund dividend checks issued each year. The checks, given to all eligible Alaskans, can be more than $1,000. These give the Alaskan economy a yearly $3 billion boost.

Arctic research is an important activity in the north. The University of Alaska's Geophysical Institute near Fairbanks carries on

What Alaska Grows, Manufactures, and Mines

Agriculture	Manufacturing	Mining
Salmon	Food products	Natural gas
Shellfish	Petroleum products	Petroleum
Vegetables	Wood products	Zinc

Alaska Permanent Fund

Many Alaskans felt the legislators spent the $900 million from the original oil leases unwisely. To compensate, the state took the first $900 million of money that came in from their share of the oil sales and created a permanent trust fund. Governor Jay Hammond believed that the oil belonged to the people of Alaska and that they should share in its sale. He proposed that each year, part of the profits from the trust fund be paid to Alaska's citizens at the rate of $50 for each year they had lived in the state, up to twenty years. Newcomer-to-the-state lawyer Ron Zobel sued, claiming that the fund discriminated against newcomers. Three years later, Zobel won his suit, and now all eligible Alaskans receive equal checks drawn from 25 percent of the profits of the fund. The Alaska Permanent Fund has grown into the largest trust fund in the nation, worth more than $20 billion. ■

basic research in many areas, including global warming and aurora research, which studies solar plasma and the building blocks of life. Another kind of research is being done by drug companies. They are studying traditional Native shaman medicines and remedies and the soils on which medicinal herbs grow. The researchers and shamans hope this knowledge will help develop modern medicines.

Farmers' markets attract summer crowds.

Farming

Although Alaska has about 15 million acres (6 million ha) of farmable land, only about 1 million acres (0.4 million ha) are farmed. Farmers find it difficult to compete with cheaply produced food shipped north. The Matanuska Valley farms provide dairy products and, in summer, fresh vegetables for much of the state. In the twenty-four-hour

Where Alaska Gets Its Energy and Water

Two-thirds of Alaska's electricity comes from natural gas. The rest comes from hydroelectric dams (14 percent), oil (13 percent), and coal (7 percent).

Tap water comes from rivers, lakes, and springs around the state. Despite all the water in the state, water is still precious in many areas such as the North Slope, with its scant precipitation. In some villages, water is hand-carried or delivered by truck to a cistern. Even in remote Alaska, water from rivers and lakes must be treated before being used.

Anchorage gets its water from Lake Eklutna in the nearby mountains, which is fed by glacier- and snowmelt. The water is brought into town by a gravity-controlled pipeline. In 1998, at the national mayors' conference, 161 mayors blind tested the drinking water from their cities. They voted Anchorage's the best-tasting. ■

summer daylight, some crops quickly grow to enormous size, especially cold weather crops such as lettuce, broccoli, carrots, potatoes, and peas. Cabbages grow to 90 pounds (41 kg) and turnips to 30 pounds (14 kg). Barley from the Interior feeds live-stock and is sometimes shipped to Asia.

Tourism

Each year, millions of people from around the world visit Alaska. Many are eco- or cultural tourists coming to see the magnificent unspoiled land, the animals in the wild, and Native villages. Some tourists are adventurers coming to climb mountains, raft white

Tourist attractions in Homer

water rivers, run marathon races, and test themselves against nature. Some are sportspeople coming for the world-class hunting and fish-ing. Some are photographers hunting for the photograph of their lives. Some just come to look around and breathe fresh air. More and more, tourists are coming in the winter for great skiing, dogsledding, winter carnivals, the northern lights, and the fun of being in a cold place.

Most tourists fly into An-chorage and travel on to other

Tourists' Top-Ten-Most-Visited Places

1. Southeastern Inside Passage—the waterway from Ketchikan to Skagway
2. Portage Glacier—south of Anchorage
3. Mendenhall Glacier—outside of Juneau
4. Ketchikan Totems
5. Denali National Park (above)
6. Skagway's Historical Gold Rush District
7. Glacier Bay—Southeastern Alaska
8. Anchorage Museum of History and Art
9. Trans-Alaska Pipeline
10. Sitka's St. Michael's Russian Orthodox Church ■

points, or drive up the Alaskan Highway, or take a cruise ship or the Alaska state ferry through Southeastern Alaska. But no matter the purpose or method, all tourists seem to have great adventures.

....

Economic Leaders

Robert Atwood, Journalist

Bob Atwood came to Alaska from Massachusetts as a journalist. In the early 1930s, he bought a small failing newspaper and turned it into the state's major newspaper. He worked tirelessly for statehood and economic development and won the first Alaskan of the Year award. As philanthropists, he and his wife, a historian and writer, funded a special journalism professorship at the University of Alaska at Anchorage, financed a theater in the new performing arts center, and donated a great deal of money to other Alaskan causes.

Dave Rose, Investment Advisor

The army brought Dave Rose to Alaska from his home in New York City. Like so many military people, he decided to stay. He had received a degree in accounting from Queens College and became comptroller of the U.S. Army in Alaska. In his study to reduce costs, he found 3,500 jobs he considered could be eliminated. When he was finished, he added his own to the list.

While working to establish more parks in Anchorage, Rose decided to run for city council, where he served many years. He later served as the first director of the Permanent Fund. Under his direction, the state fund grew from $900 million to more than $12 billion in ten years. Now Rose heads a private investment advisory company and is overseeing the investment of the Aleut internment settlement fund. ■

Work for the Future

One of Alaska's new growth industries is air cargo service. Alaska sits on the central northern edge of the Pacific Rim, about halfway between Europe and Asia and the East Coast and Asia. This makes it the perfect refueling place for global air traffic. Today, with the popularity of overnight international air-cargo services, Anchorage

Merrill Field, an airport in downtown Anchorage

has more cargo passing through it than any other American city. Most major carriers have headquarters in Anchorage, where they sort and ship cargo.

Alaska is also playing an important role in the economic development of Russia. It is the staging area for eastern Russia's oil and gold exploration and for U.S. companies' business development there. Alaska also participates in educational, cultural, and economic exchanges with Russia.

The Red Dog Zinc Mine

In 1953, while flying more than 90 miles (145 km) north of Kotzebue, prospector Bob Baker noticed a red stain on the land. Tests confirmed it was a zinc, lead, and silver deposit. The entire area became known as Red Dog, named for Baker's companion and copilot, his red dog.

That deposit is the largest open-pit zinc mine and reserve in the world. It is a joint venture between the NANA Native Corporation, which owns the land, and Cominco, a Canadian mining company. As part of the agreement, qualified Natives have priority for jobs and the development must be environmentally safe. Today, water runoff from the mine has zero contaminants and is far purer than the original water, which is too toxic for fish.

Each year the mine produces 600,000 metric tons of zinc and 90,000 tons of lead concentrate. Soon the mine will expand production by 40 percent. Red Dog zinc is shipped all around the world for many uses ranging from coating steel to prevent rust to making vitamins. ■

CHAPTER NINE

Who Are Those Alaskans?

A young Yup'ik Inuit dancer

Alaska—an unusual and spacious land—attracts many unusual people. Almost more than anything, Alaskans value individualism and independence. Perhaps this springs from the ruggedness of the land and those people who came to Alaska when it was a difficult place to live. These include Alaskan Natives who survived and thrived in the harshest conditions, the eager gold rushers who believed in optimism in all situations, and the can-do attitude of those who built the Alaskan Highway and the oil pipeline when it was considered nearly impossible. Today, Alaska is a much kinder place to live, but the virtues of those pioneers are the foundation of the state's personality. Alaska today reflects both youthful energy and excitement of newcomers and ancient wisdom of its Native elders.

Facts and Figures about Alaskans

Although Alaska is the largest state, with only 626,932 people in 2000 it is the third least populated and the least densely populated. Alaska has about 1 person for each square mile of land. The entire United States has 79 people per square mile. Alaska is a rapidly growing state. In 1970, there were only 300,000 people there.

The people of Alaska are among the youngest and best educated in the nation. The average age is 32.4 years but is rising

Opposite: The Palmer State Fair

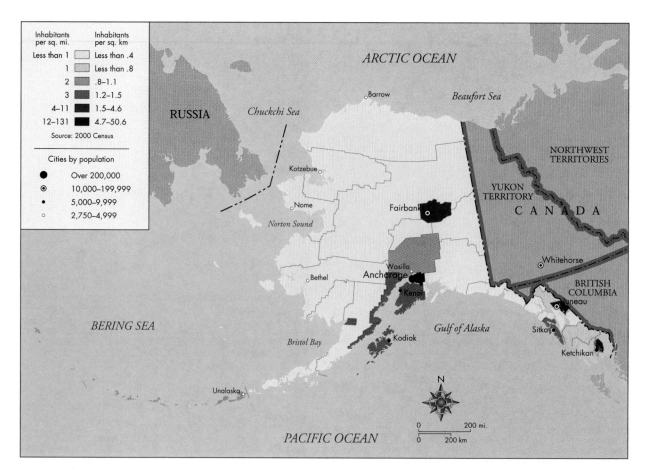

Map legend:

Inhabitants per sq. mi.		Inhabitants per sq. km
Less than 1		Less than .4
1		Less than .8
2		.8–1.1
3		1.2–1.5
4–11		1.5–4.6
12–131		4.7–50.6

Source: 2000 Census

Cities by population

- ● Over 200,000
- ◉ 10,000–199,999
- • 5,000–9,999
- ○ 2,750–4,999

Alaska's population density by borough

Population of Alaska's Major Cities (2000)

Anchorage	260,283
Juneau	30,711
Fairbanks	30,224
Sitka	8,835
Ketchikan	7,922

because the state has one of the fastest growing senior populations. Contrary to stories about Alaska being short of women, the population is about equally divided between men and women.

About 69 percent of Alaskans are white. Natives make up about 16 percent of the population, and the rest is about evenly divided between African-Americans, Hispanics, and Asians and Pacific Islanders. The majority of Natives live in rural villages, although their number in cities is increasing. Most nonnatives live in cities or small towns. More than 100 languages are spoken in the state. Many Native languages are spoken in homes, taught in schools, and used in village businesses.

Citrus Broiled Alaska Salmon

Salmon is one of Alaska's most sought-after exports. Here is a simple, tasty recipe for this delicious fish.

Ingredients:
   2 oranges
   4 Alaska salmon fillets (4 to 6 oz. each),
      thawed if necessary
   salt to taste
   1 tsp. red wine vinegar
   1/4 cup sliced green onions
   1 tsp. cracked black pepper

Directions:

Slice peel and pith from oranges; slice cross-wise into 1/4 inch rounds.

Season salmon fillets with salt. Broil fillets 4 to 6 inches from heat, allowing 10 minutes per inch of thickness, measured at the thickest part.

Remove fillets just before they are cooked through.

Sprinkle with vinegar.

Arrange orange rounds on top, and sprinkle with green onions and cracked pepper. Broil 1 minute longer.

Makes 4 servings.

City Life and Village Life

City life in Alaska is much like life anywhere else. Mostly school and jobs fill the days. Family, activities, homework, and sports fill the evenings. Although it is a four- or five-day drive to the closest state, the Internet, cell and regular phones, and satellite television tie Alaska to the rest of the country.

Life in villages is slower paced than hectic city schedules, and the sense of community is stronger. Everyone knows one another, and a good share of the town is probably related. But even remote villages without electricity aren't isolated: Houses usually have gas-powered generators that can run a computer and a television.

Humanitarians

Life can be hard in Alaska, especially in winter. People come from the Lower 48 expecting high-paying jobs and instead find high-priced housing and food and no jobs. For people arriving in the cities from rural Alaska, the noise, traffic, and strangers can be disorienting.

Living in Cold Weather

Alaskans are northerners. Those who have been in the state awhile like winter. It is the norm and a relief from the hectic days of summer. Cold days can be a pleasure. People are usually well prepared for cold. They often own more coats, mittens, gloves, and hats than southerners have shorts and sandals. People carry tow-ropes and shovels in their cars in case they get stuck in the snow. In extreme cold, they leave cars running while they shop, because the vehicles can be difficult to restart in the frigid weather.

The most cases of frostbite at one time do not happen in the most extreme cold weather, though. Fairbanks often suffers –50°F (–45°C) for weeks. When it suddenly warms up to –10°F (–23°C) overnight, it feels so wonderfully warm, people go outside to celebrate the coming spring too long without hats, mittens, or warm jackets.

Young Alaskan Natives seem to be conditioned against the extreme cold. Even at –20°F (–2°C) they comfortably play outside in light jackets. ■

Many organizations help those having a tough time. Three especially well-known humanitarians are Michael O'Callaghan, "Mother" Alice Lawrence, and Archbishop Francis Hurley. O'Callaghan, a *Newsweek* local hero, is known for his impatience. He and his organization, EARTH, don't wait for things to be studied: They make them happen. O'Callaghan is best known for getting food to people and has organized dozens of fish giveaways. With donated labor and equipment, thousands of surplus hatchery salmon are iced, shipped to a town, and handed out to anyone who shows up.

First Lady Hillary Clinton with Mother Alice Lawrence

Mother Lawrence takes care of whomever comes to her door, whether this entails giving them clothes, food, time, or money. The people of Anchorage recently built her a larger home to better accommodate all the people she feeds. In 1997, President and Mrs. Clinton honored her at a White House luncheon.

Catholic Archbishop Hurley and the City of Anchorage joined together to build and operate the free Beans Café and Brother Francis Shelter for those in need. Restaurants, businesses, churches, and townspeople donate food, time, and money to help provide food and a refuge from the streets. These three people represent the generous hearts of people all over Alaska.

High school students learning algebra via satellite TV

Education

Just as in the rest of the United States, most young Alaskans get up in the morning, walk to the bus stop, and ride to their neighborhood public school. Occasionally, a moose might browse near the stop. In school, most of the time they study what all American students study. Some schools have specialized programs such as art-based education or language-immersion. In some village schools, the language class may be in Yup'ik, Inupiat, or Tlingit, and the classes after recess consist of Native crafts such as ivory carving, skin sewing, or beadwork.

Children in remote areas often study by correspondence courses offered by the state. Some rural schools get special courses and lectures from other schools by teleconference or satellite. Most schools, village and town, use computers and the Internet extensively.

Students living in small villages of only a few hundred people used to have to go to boarding school after eighth grade. Molly Hooch was one of these. She did not want to leave her home and family, so eventually Alaska Legal Services filed a lawsuit against the state on behalf of her and others like her. Because children are required to attend school until they are fifteen, the suit claimed the state should provide schools for them in their home communities. An out-of-court settlement sparked the building of many small high schools in villages throughout the state. Students now have a choice of traveling to Mount Edgecumbe boarding school in Sitka or studying in their own village. These one- and two-room high schools double as community centers and occasionally have the only electricity and running water in town.

Alaska has three colleges: the University of Alaska system, which has many branches and distance learning throughout the state; and two highly regarded

The Juneau campus of the University of Alaska

Alaska Talk

Break-up The spring thaw

Camai A Native word meaning hello, welcome, good-bye, and come again. Similar to Hawaii's *aloha.*

Cheechako A newcomer, especially someone who has yet to spend an entire winter in Alaska

Lower 48 The contiguous 48 states

Mukluks Very warm pull-on winter boots traditionally made of seal or reindeer skin and fur

Muktuk The outer edge of whale blubber which is considered by many a great delicacy

Outside Anyplace not Alaska. During the gold rush, most people sailed up Southeastern's Inside Passage to Alaska. To return home, they were going back down the Inside to the Outside.

Sourdough An old-timer, someone who has been in Alaska for many years. The term comes from the gold rush days when sourdough starter used to make bread was always carried around.

Termination dust The first dusting of snow on the mountains that signals the end of summer and of summer work. ■

liberal arts colleges, Alaska Pacific University and Sheldon Jackson College. The Fairbanks branch of the University of Alaska is strong in the field of science and focuses on many areas of Arctic research. The largest branch, in Anchorage, attracts students from forty-nine countries.

Do the Inuit Really Have Twenty Different Words for Snow?

Yes, and more. The words describe different kinds of snow. Old snow, fresh snow, snow for melting into drinking water, snow the texture of corn, snow the texture of rice, falling snow, fallen snow, dry snow, wet snow, snowdrift, snowstorm, snowflake, packed snow, fluffy snow, covered with snow, crusted snow, crystallized snow, wavy surface of drifting snow, overhanging snow, little snow, snow cliff, and more. There are nearly as many words for ice. ■

Life in Scammon Bay

Many people might think the tundra village of Scammon Bay is at the end of the world and an odd place to live. Indeed, it does lie beside the Kun River, at the base of the Askinuk Mountains, a mile from the Bering Sea and far from the world's road system. But 425 people, mostly Yup'ik, think it is a pretty great place to live. Most of their ancestors have lived there for thousands of years.

A typical family in this subsistence village might have several generations living together or close by. About 40 percent of parents and grandparents have regular jobs. Others hunt, fish, preserve food, or create craft items for sale such as woven grassbaskets, beadwork, or skin mukluks. Because most supplies must be barged up from the Lower 48 during the summer, they don't consider many material items, such as heavy furniture, necessary for a good life.

An important part of the good life in Scammon Bay is visiting. Children meet at the store to buy bubble gum and chat. Adults share news and gossip at the post office. Everyone goes house to house for tea and talk.

The Council of Elders has worked hard to keep Scammon Bay a good place to live. They have arranged for the installation of electricity, indoor plumbing, and running water. There is a town gymnasium, a health clinic, and school for the 129 students. However, there are no real roads—trails weave from house to house, school to store. People travel by all-terrain vehicle or snowmobile. Alcohol is absolutely not allowed in Scammon Bay. Anyone reporting smugglers can earn $1,000.

Elders have the responsibility to pass along life skills, ideals, and stories of the Yup'ik people to the young. Young people learn both traditional and new ways. They are as comfortable using a computer as skinning a seal, as comfortable performing story dances as swishing a basketball.

The whole town loves basketball and everyone turns out to cheer for the boys' and girls' teams. For away games, everyone caravans by snowmobile across the tundra to nearby villages. Even on snowmobiles, winter nights can be warm and pleasant. Moonlight glows off the snow. Overhead stars fill the

sky. Some nights the Northern Lights play across the horizon and the mountains stand white against the deep blue sky.

When summer comes the air is thick with the scent of salt. The sky, a thin blue, barely the color of the sea, is full of migrating birds. Many of the Yup'ik people move to their fish camp and spend a month catching, cleaning, and drying fish during the day. At night they dance, tell stories, and talk about family members long gone. They remember all the good things, all the important memories to take to the future. And they all know why Scammon Bay, at the end of the world, is indeed a great place to live. ■

CHAPTER TEN

Alaskan Art and Alaskan Fun

Yup'ik baskets

Everyone agrees: Mother Nature is the best artist in Alaska. Her wonderful work is a powerful and continual draw for painters, sculptors, writers, performers, weavers, musicians, and dancers hungry for inspiration. Everyone, residents and visitors alike, is so overwhelmed by this giant land, it seems to find its way into nearly every painting, sculpture, poem, song, and dance.

Alaska draws creative people from around the country to study and perform in its splendid settings. The Sitka Summer Music Festival, Valdez Playwriting Workshop, Fairbanks Midnight Sun Writers Conference, and the Fairbanks Arts Camp for Children all offer top quality instructors and performers.

Alaska, like most frontier communities, values the cultural arts. All types of music fill the Alaskan air, from garage bands to Native walrus-skin drums to the energetic Athabascan fiddlers to fine symphony orchestras. Galleries line downtown streets. And everyone argues about the merits of the latest public art project. With the first oil money, Anchorage voted to invest in several modern buildings and earmark 1 percent of the building cost for art. The city tripled the size of the museum, built a performing arts center, a convention center, a sports arena, and an elegant library, each full of sculptures, paintings, and functional art.

Opposite: Detail of a totem pole in Ketchikan

Sydney Laurence

Painter Sydney
Laurence came north
during the gold rush.
He had studied painting
in Europe but had not
found fame or fortune
in art, so he turned to
gold mining. At the
first sight of Mount
McKinley, he became
so enthralled, he gave
up gold mining and
concentrated on paint-
ing the mountain over
and over in every light,
in every season. Miners
enthusiastically bought
his landscape paintings
to remember the moun-
tain they could never
forget, and Laurence
found his fame and
fortune. ■

Because of Anchorage's position as a refueling stop for
continental airplanes, many top shows and performers flying
from the East Coast of the United States or Europe to Asia stop
there for a few days to rest and perform. As a result, Anchorage
has a range of entertainment opportunities that no other town its
size enjoys.

Native Art

Alaskans have a prehistoric tradition of creating works of art from
nature. Among the most magnificent are Hooper Bay grass baskets.
The weaving in these baskets is so fine, it resembles satin. Inupiat
men weave whale-baleen baskets. The baleen is so difficult to
work, only men with very strong hands can manage it. Native
carvers and sculptors have long used wood, bone, soapstone, jade,
feathers, ivory, and metals for their sculptures, masks, and deco-
rations. Other special traditional works are the Tlingit blankets,
Athabascan beadwork, and skin sewing.

Dancing is a traditional mode of storytelling in all Native
communities. Most villages have professional dance troupes that
perform and compete in Alaska, the United States, and around the
world.

Winter Art

Like many northern communities, Alaska makes excellent use of
some of its most abundant raw materials for art—snow and ice
sculptures. People decorate their yards and towns with these tran-
sitory artworks. In Anchorage's town square, ice sculptures replace

The Anchorage Historical and Fine Arts Museum

The exterior of the Anchorage Museum is a work of art in itself. Slate inlays pattern the sidewalk. Yards and yards of brilliant flowers border the walkways in summer. "Crystal Lattice," a sculpture by Robert Pfitzenmeier, graces the entrance courtyard. Outside, above the entry doors, is a giant mosaic owl titled *The Intruder*, by Ned Smyth.

Inside are three distinct exhibits. The lower level highlights art, with permanent collections and visiting exhibits, including the Alaska collection and the contemporary Native artists collection. In a separate wing, the children's section rotates hands-on exhibits, displays, and activities.

Upstairs, the exhibits trace Alaska's history from the first land bridge crossings until the present. Visitors walk around Inuit, Aleut, Athabascan, and Tlingit homes. Nearby are a Russian blockhouse, a gold-prospector's cabin, and an early pioneer farmhouse. A large moose walks through the farmhouse's backyard. There are exhibits of Native carvings, Russian artifacts, gold displays, a section of the pipeline, oil-spill-cleaning equipment, and the robes worn by Pope John Paul II when he visited the city. Cases lining the balcony walls display logbooks and drawings from the first European explorers and photographs and histories of pioneer families. ■

summer flowers. Fairbanks hosts a sculpturing competition that draws competitors from around the world. Lawn sculptures range from a life-size nativity scene at Christmas to a life-size polar bear guarding the front door.

A sculpture at the Ice Art Festival in Fairbanks

Jewel Kilcher

Jewel Kilcher, known to her fans simply as Jewel, grew up near Homer without electricity or running water. As a girl, she began singing with her family. She loved being outdoors and running in the wilderness. The forests, mountains, and ocean were part of her childhood until she left for college in California.

There she performed nightly in small clubs. As word spread about the girl who could sing, an Atlantic Records official heard her and offered her a contract. After that she spent months traveling throughout the country in a van and performing her signature song, "Who Will Save Your Soul?" to build up name recognition. Her determination and tireless work paid off. Her CD became a megahit. She won best new artist awards and joined the elite of popular and successful musical artists. She has published a best-selling book of poetry and released another album. ■

Writers

The movement of the sun, moon, stars, and auroras across the Alaskan sky is a form of poetry, so naturally Alaska spawns many poets, writers, and essayists. They often find their settings and themes in the Alaskan scenery and in humankind's ability to challenge nature.

A Spiritual Landmark

Of all the famous landmarks in Alaska—the totems of Ketchikan, the state capital building in Juneau, the life-size Last Blue Whale sculpture in Anchorage, the Captain Cook statue standing at the edge of Cook Inlet, or the pipeline rising out of the ground near Fairbanks— probably the most interesting is the whalebone arch standing at the edge of the Arctic Ocean near Barrow. Two great whale jawbones lean together like a cathedral door open to the sea. Many tourists, looking very small, pose for pictures standing in the great arched whale jaw, ocean and ice at their back. ■

Alaska takes its poetry seriously, even fun poetry, like Anchorage's two day Poetry Slam, where poetry, performance art, and humor blend. Alaska is home to national award-winning poet Linda McCarriston and poet laureate Tom Sexton, as well as many excellent writers in all genres.

Sports in Alaska

Alaska is meant for fun. People come from all over the world to climb her mountains and raft her wild rivers. In a state where the outdoors is so vast, naturally sports is an important part of everyday life. Because each summer day lasts most of the night, too, the days have room for hiking, in-line skating, baseball, basketball, tennis, soccer, golf, fishing, boating, and more. Those too impatient for winter add wheels to their cross-country skis and dogsleds and train all summer long.

Because winter covers so many months, there is plenty of time for skiing, snowshoeing, snowboarding, ice-climbing, skating, and

Traditional Games

Alaskans enjoy playing a variety of Native historical games. Some evolved practically, such as the blanket toss (left), which propelled a spotter into the air to look for game across the tundra. Some were meant for fun, such as the ear pull. In the ear pull, a cord loop is placed around two opposing competitors' ears. In an ear-tug-of-war, the two contenders try to pull each other off balance. Some games build strength and agility, such as the one- and two-legged high kicks. A small ball is suspended from above: the athlete, from a standing position, tries to kick the ball. The best athletes can kick 2 to 3 feet (0.6 to 1 m) above their heads. ■

Snowshoe softball

hockey. All winter long, people too impatient for summer play snow football, snow soccer, snow golf, and snow basketball on snow-covered outdoor fields.

Almost all sports enjoyed in the rest of the United States are played in Alaska, even waterskiing and lake swimming, although children in northern villages sometimes wear survival suits. There are sports special to Alaska—mostly Native games such as the leg kick, knuckle walk, and blanket toss.

As much as Alaskans like participating in sports, they also enjoy watching top athletes, especially Alaska's college and semi-professional baseball, basketball, and hockey teams. More than 100 major league baseball players, including Mark McGwire and

Randy Johnson, started with Alaska's semipro teams. Watching and playing hockey is so popular with both boys and girls that indoor ice rinks are reserved for games and practices from very early in the morning until late at night. Most schools have an outdoor ice rink. A popular spectator event is the grueling 365-mile (587-km) wheelchair race from Fairbanks to Anchorage.

Basketball is a natural for Alaskan winters. It is especially popular in the villages. Magic Johnson, Isiah Thomas, and Karl Malone have lead youth clinics in Barrow, and all expressed surprise at the students' skills, especially Thomas, who was beaten in one-on-one play. Alaskans schools continually turn out dedicated players. Anchorage's Trajan Langdon played on the U.S. All-Star High School team, the U.S. Olympic team, and seems destined for the National Basketball Association (NBA). Each Thanksgiving, seven top college teams from around the nation come to Anchorage to play against the University of Alaska there in the Great Alaska Shootout, a season-opening tournament.

Alaska's training programs in Nordic and Alpine skiing, skating, and snowboarding have turned out top Olympic athletes such as ski champion gold medalist Tommy Moe and silver medalist Hillary Lindh.

Many national and international winter games have been held in Alaska. The World Extreme Skiing Championships are in Valdez each April, and the World Eskimo and Indian Olympics are held each July in Fairbanks. Alaska has also hosted the International Arctic Winter Games and international Nordic skiing and snowboarding competitions. The winter World Special Olympics was also held in Anchorage in 2001.

Inupiat dance
drummers at the
World Eskimo Indian
Olympics

Dogsled Racing

Dogsleds were a vital part of winter transportation until the invention of the snowmobile. Since then, dogsledding has developed into a popular sport around the world. The racing dogs, mostly malamutes and Siberian huskies, are like Thoroughbred horses: They love running. When they see the racing harnesses, they jump and yelp with excitement. Often, the mushers' most difficult task is to make the dogs wait for the start. Many kinds of races are held around the state, even short ones for children and puppies. But the most popular and challenging of all races is the Iditarod.

The Iditarod Race—"The Last Great Race on Earth"

The Iditarod race exists because of two people's efforts. Dorothy Page and Joe Redington both loved mushing and preserving the old trails across Alaska. When the army cleared and marked the old northern trail in 1972, they began to organize an Anchorage to

Nome race. The Iditarod race begins in downtown Anchorage and travels 1,100 miles (1,770 km) across wild country to Nome. Mushers come from around the world to compete. For safety reasons, a team must pass many tests before participating.

The Anchorage to Eagle River portion of the race has become largely ceremonial. Sponsors ride in sleds through town, and people line the streets and trails wishing the teams a good journey. The next day, the race restarts at Willow, 40 miles (64 km) north of Anchorage, with packed sleds. Extra supplies are airlifted to checkpoints along the trail.

Thousands of volunteers help with the race, from corporate sponsors to prison inmates who care for dogs left at checkpoints, to schoolchildren who adopt a musher. Around the country, classes support a musher by writing letters of encouragement, making hundreds of booties to protect the dogs' feet in icy conditions, and watching their musher's progress on the Internet.

In 1973, Dick Wilmarth won the first race in twenty days. After winning, his lead dog, Hot Foot, got loose. Wilmarth finally found him waiting at home in Red Devil, 500 miles (805 km) away. With training and trail improvements, now the race is routinely won in nine to twelve days. Doug Swingley, from Montana, holds the record of 9 days, 2 hours, 42 minutes, and 19 seconds. Yes, seconds matter. One year, after two weeks on the trail, only one second separated first and second place.

As each musher, first to last, comes onto Front Street in Nome, a siren sounds and, night or day, people come to cheer the team. It may take three weeks or longer for the Red Lantern winner, last

Opposite: An Iditarod dogsled musher leaving the starting gate

A Far and Distant Place

In 1908, gold was discovered near *Haiditarod*, the Native word for "a far and distant place." By the time the gold disappeared and most of its 20,000 residents had moved on, Iditarod had become a main stop on the trail system across western Alaska.

In January 1925, Nome had an outbreak of diphtheria, known as black death. Dogsled was the only practical means to transport serum to Nome, but it would likely take fifteen days, and people would die waiting. The 20-pound (9-kg) package went by train from Anchorage to Nenana and then was relayed from musher to musher toward Nome. Those people planning to wait for fifteen days didn't count on the courage and stamina of lead dogs such as Balto and Togo or mushers such as Leonhard Seppela and Gunner Kasson. These and other teams raced through blizzards with wind chills of −100°F (−73°C) to deliver the serum to Nome in five-and-a-half days. Today, there is a statue of Balto in New York City's Central Park and a very popular animated film about his life (above). ■

Women Mushers

Many women mush dogs, but three names are synonymous with success in long-distance mushing: Libby Riddles, Susan Butcher (above), and Dee Dee Jonrowe. Riddles was the first woman to win the Iditarod. She took risks men wouldn't when she left the last checkpoint before Nome during a tremendous blizzard. Other mushers thought they would have to organize a search party, but she was waiting for them at the finish line. Susan Butcher has dedicated much of her life to good dog care and the race, winning four times. She recently took a break to have a baby. Dee Dee Jonrowe holds the record for the fastest woman and the fourth-fastest time ever. She's consistently a top finisher and winner of sportsperson and humanitarian awards. In 1998, high school senior Kimarie Hanson became the youngest person to finish the race. These women are all respected for their strength, determination, dog care, sportsmanship, and kind hearts. They inspired the T-shirt ALASKA—WHERE MEN ARE MEN AND WOMEN WIN THE IDITAROD. ■

place, to finish. The Red Lantern Award honors the musher's determination to finish one of the most difficult sporting events in the world.

Fun and Games

Dogsled races have become the center point of many winter festivals around the state, including Anchorage's Fur Rendezvous, which hosts the World Championship races. Fur Rendezvous, held in February, was originally when miners and trappers came into town to sell their gold and furs and celebrate. It is now one of the top ten festivals in the United States. No matter what the temperature is, it includes hundreds of activities—fireworks, an outdoor carnival, blanket toss, softball played on snowshoes, a costume ball, the 5-K Frostbite Footrace, a parade, hot air balloons, concerts and plays, art and photography shows, ice bowling, the Rondy Grand Prix Car Race, and even cribbage and chess tournaments.

Alaskans enthusiastically celebrate many things besides winter, including Cinco de Mayo, Octoberfest, and St. Patrick's Day. Fairbanks celebrates the summer solstice with a baseball game played outside at midnight, without lights of course! One of the most eagerly awaited events is the Nenana Ice Classic. In Nenana, a tripod connected to a

A Fur Rendezvous celebrant's hat shows off his trapping skills

trip wire is frozen into the river ice. Come spring, people around the state bet on the exact minute the ice will break and begin to flow. This causes the trip wire to set off an alarm, stop a clock, and signal that spring has officially arrived.

Then, once again, Alaskans will watch sunrises beside sunsets on the northern horizons. And the long summer days will be full of Alaskan activities: Fishing for salmon with a moose across the river and a bear downstream; watching the mountains change color throughout the day and night; wakening in the fresh air and hearing the birds sing; standing on a mountain top and seeing the land spread broad and distant before you, like all the possibilities in the world. These delights, and many more, make Alyeska the truly Great Land the Natives saw thousands of years ago from the land bridge across the stormy northern sea.

Finding peace in the beauty of Alaska

Timeline

United States History

The first permanent British settlement is established in North America at Jamestown.	**1607**
Pilgrims found Plymouth Colony, the second permanent British settlement.	**1620**
America declares its independence from England.	**1776**
The Treaty of Paris officially ends the Revolutionary War in America.	**1783**
The U.S. Constitution is written.	**1787**
Louisiana Purchase almost doubles the size of the United States.	**1803**
United States and Britain fight the War of 1812.	**1812–15**
The North and South fight each other in the American Civil War.	**1861–65**

Alaska State History

1741	Danish explorer Vitus Bering and German naturalist George Steller arrive in what is now Alaska and claim it for Russia.
1778	Alaska's coastline is charted by Captain James Cook of England.
1854	Russia offers to sell Alaska to the United States after the Crimean War.
1867	The United States purchases Alaska for $7.2 million.
1877	Alaska suffers when the U.S. military leaves the territory; only customs agents and three postmasters remain as government officials.
1884	Congress passes the Organic Act of Alaska, giving the territory a governor, code of laws, court personnel, and a school system.
1896	George Carmack and his two Indian partners discover gold in a tributary of the Klondike River.

United States History

The United States is **1917–18** involved in World War I.

The Stock market crashes, **1929** plunging the United States into the Great Depression.

The United States **1941–45** fights in World War II.
The United States becomes a **1945** charter member of the U.N.

The United States **1951–53** fights in the Korean War.

The U.S. Congress enacts a series of **1964** groundbreaking civil rights laws.

The United States **1964–73** engages in the Vietnam War.

The United States and other **1991** nations fight the brief Persian Gulf War against Iraq.

Alaska State History

1935 Two hundred families flock to Alaska when the U.S. government offers farmland to Americans at inexpensive prices.

1942 Japan attacks the Aleutian Islands, bombing Dutch Harbor and invading Attu and Kiska Island.
President Roosevelt orders the building of the Alaska Highway, which connects Fairbanks, Alaska to Dawson Creek, British Columbia in Canada.

1959 Alaska becomes the 49th state of the union (January 3).

1964 Southern Alaska suffers an earthquake that is the largest to ever hit North America and that kills 131 people (March 27).

1967 The Tanana Basin, which includes Fairbanks, is flooded because of heavy rains during the summer; thousands of people are evacuated to higher ground.

1967 The largest oil field on U.S. land is discovered at Prudhoe Bay.

1977 Oil begins flowing through the Trans-Alaska Pipeline, which is more than 800 miles (487 km) long.

1989 An oil supertanker, the *Exxon Valdez*, hits a reef in Prince William Sound and spills 11 million gallons (42 million l) of oil into the water. It is the worst spill in U.S. history

Fast Facts

The capitol

Statehood date	January 3, 1959, the 49th state
Origin of state name	From the Aleut word meaning "mainland" or "great land"
State capital	Juneau
State nickname	Last Frontier, Land of the Midnight Sun
State motto	"North to the future"
State bird	Willow ptarmigan
State flower	Forget-me-not
State fish	King salmon
State mineral	Gold
State gem	Jade
State insect	Four-spot skimmer dragonfly
State land mammal	Moose
State marine mammal	Bowhead whale
State sport	Dog sled racing (mushing)
State song	"Alaska's Flag"
State tree	Sitka spruce
State fair	Palmer (August)

Gold

Mount McKinley

Total area; rank	615,230 sq. mi. (1,593,445 sq km); 1st
Land; rank	570,374 sq. mi. (1,477,268 sq km); 1st
Water; rank	44,856 sq. mi. (116,177 sq km); 1st
Inland water; **rank**	17,501 sq. mi. (45,327 sq km); 1st
Coastal water; **rank**	27,355 sq. mi. (70,849 sq km); 1st
Geographic center	60 miles (97 km) northwest of Mt. McKinley, 63° 50′ N, 152° W
Latitude and longitude	Alaska is located approximately between 52° 00′ and 74° 00′ N and 130° 00′ and 172° E
Highest point	Mount McKinley, 20,320 feet (6,194 m)
Lowest point	Sea level at the Pacific Ocean
Largest city	Anchorage
Organized boroughs	16
Population; rank	626,932 (2000 census); 48th
Density	109 persons per 100 sq. mi. (42 per 100 sq. km)
Population distribution	67% urban, 33% rural

Ethnic distribution (does not equal 100%)

White	69.3%
Native American	15.6%
African-American	3.5%
Hispanic	4.1%
Asian and Pacific Islanders	4.0%
Other	1.6%

Record high temperature	100°F (38°C) at Fort Yukon on June 27, 1915
Record low temperature	−80°F (−62°C) at Prospect Creek, near Stevens Village, on January 23, 1971

At the Palmer State Fair

Growing alfalfa

Average July temperature	55°F (13°C)
Average January temperature	5°F (−15°C)
Average annual precipitation	Varies from 5 inches (13 cm) in the Arctic to 300 inches (762 cm) along the southern coast

Natural Areas and Historic Sites

National Parks and Preserves

Bering Land Bridge National Preserve is the remnant of the land bridge that connected North America to Asia more than 13,000 years ago.

Denali National Park and Preserve contains Mount McKinley, North America's highest peak.

Gates of the Arctic National Park and Preserve contains archaeological records of human habitation as long as 10,000 years ago.

Glacier Bay National Park and Preserve contains great tidewater glaciers as well as a wide variety of animal life.

Katmai National Park and Preserve is the site of active volcanic vents at the Valley of Ten Thousand Smokes.

Lake Clark National Park and Preserve includes two active volcanoes, Mount Redoubt and Mount Iliamna.

Wrangell–Saint Elias National Park and Preserve is the largest unit of the National Park System and includes three mountain ranges, North America's second highest peak, Mount Saint Elias, and many glaciers.

National Parks

Kenai Fjords National Park contains the Harding icefield, one of the four major ice caps in the United States.

Kobuk Valley National Park contains evidence of 10,000 years of human habitation, as well as diverse wildlife.

Denali National Park

Sitka National Park

Tongass National Forest

National Preserves

Noatak National Preserve contains the largest mountain-ringed river basin in the United States and is still virtually untouched by humans.

Yukon-Charley Rivers National Preserve protects part of the Yukon River and all of the Charley River basin.

National Historical Parks

Klondike Gold Rush National Historical Park memorializes the 1897–98 gold rush.

Sitka National Historical Park is the site of a fort and the battle that was the last major resistance of the Tlingit people against Russian settlers.

National Monuments

Aniakchak National Monument is one of the great dry calderas, or volcanic craters, in the world, last erupting in 1931.

Cape Krusenstern National Monument is an archaeological site containing evidence of 4,000 years of human habitation.

National Forests

Alaska has the nation's two largest National Forests, *Tongass* and *Chugach.* Tongass National Forest encompasses 17 million acres (7 million ha) and Chugach National Park covers 5.6 million acres (2.3 million ha).

State Parks

Alaska began establishing its state park system in the 1960s. Today, it includes recreation areas, trails, and historic sites.

Sports Teams

NCAA Hockey Teams (Division I)

UAA Seawolves and UAF Nanooks

WHCL Team

Anchorage Aces

University of Alaska Southeast

Cultural Institutions

Libraries

The Alaska State Library (Juneau) contains the state archives as well as historical collections on Alaska's past.

Loussac Library (Anchorage) is the largest public library and houses one of the state's most extensive Alaska book collections.

The University of Alaska-Fairbanks Library, The University of Alaska-Anchorage Library, and *The University of Alaska-Southeast Library* are all academic libraries.

Museums

The Alaska State Museum (Juneau) and *The Sheldon Jackson Museum* (Sitka) contains exhibits and objects from Inuit and American Indian cultures.

The University of Alaska Museum (Fairbanks) contains historical and wildlife exhibits as well as a collection of Alaskan art.

Performing Arts

Alaska has one major opera company as well as several fine symphonies and theater groups.

Universities and Colleges

In the mid-1990s, Alaska had three public and four private institutions of higher learning.

Annual Events

January–March

Russian Christmas, in cities across the state (early January)

Winter Sunrise in Barrow (late January)

Fur Rendezvous in Anchorage (February)

Iditarod Trail Sled Dog Race (March)

Pillar Mountain Golf Classic in Kodiak (March)

Iditarod

Eskimo-Indian Olympics

April–June

Alaska Folk Festival in Juneau (April)

Little Norway Festival in Petersburg (May)

Kodiak Crab Festival (May)

The Midnight Sun in Barrow (mid-May)

Sitka Summer Music Festival (June)

Summer solstice celebrations in cities across the state (June)

July–September

World Eskimo-Indian Olympics in Fairbanks (July)

State Fair in Palmer (August–September)

Equinox Marathon Run in Fairbanks (September)

October–December

Alaska Day Celebration in Sitka, commemorating the transfer of Alaska from Russia to the United States in 1867 (October)

Athabascan Fiddling Festival in Fairbanks (November)

Great Alaska Shootout in Anchorage, featuring college basketball teams from throughout the United States (November)

Famous People

James Cook

E. L. "Bob" Bartlett (1904–1968)	Politician
Vitus Jonassen Bering (1681–1741)	Navigator
James Cook (1728–1779)	Explorer
Anthony Joseph Dimond (1881–1953)	Politician
William Allen Egan (1914–1984)	Governor
Joseph Juneau (1826?–1890)	Gold prospector
Elizabeth Peratrovich (1911–1958)	Civil rights activist
Howard Rock (1911–1984)	Publisher and activist
Theodore Fulton Stevens (1923–)	Politician

To Find Out More

History

- Cohen, Daniel. *The Alaska Purchase*. Brookfield, Conn.: Millbrook, 1996.

- Declements, Barthe, and Dan Andreasen (illus.). *The Bite of the Gold Bug: A Story of the Alaskan Gold Rush*. New York: Puffin, 1994.

- Doherty, Craig A., and Katherine M. Doherty. *The Alaska Pipeline*. Woodbridge, Conn.: Blackbirch, 1998.

- Fradin, Dennis Brindell. *Alaska*. Chicago: Childrens Press, 1994.

- Gill, Shelley, and Shannon Cartwright (illus.). *Thunderfeet: Alaska's Dinosaurs and Other Prehistoric Critters*. Homer, Alaska: Paws IV, 1992.

- Johnston, Joyce. *Alaska*. Minneapolis: Lerner, 1994.

- Oberle, Joseph G. *Anchorage*. Parsippany, N.J.: Dillon, 1990.

- Thompson, Kathleen. *Alaska*. Austin, Tex.: Raintree/Steck Vaughn, 1996.

Fiction

- Brown, Tricia, and Roy Corral (illus.). *Children of the Midnight Sun: Young Native Voices of Alaska*. Anchorage: Alaska Northwest Books, 1998.

- George, Jean Craighead. *Julie of the Wolves*. New York: HarperCollins, 1987.
- London, Jack. *The Call of the Wild*. New York: Puffin, 1994.
- Morey, Walt, and John Schoenherr (illus.). *Gentle Ben*. New York: Puffin, 1992.

Biographies

- Noonan, Jon. *Captain Cook*. Parsippany, N.J.: Crestwood House, 1993.

Websites

- **Alaska Parks**
  http://www.alaska-online.com/parks/index.htm
  A well-designed and informative page covering national and state parks as well as wildlife refuges

- **Everything Alaska**
  http://www.everythingalaska.com/
  Contains links to information about Alaska's weather, online newspapers, state information and facts, and native links

- **State of Alaska's Home Page**
  http://www.state.ak.us
  The official website for the state with many links

Addresses

- **Division of Tourism**
  PO Box 110801
  Juneau, AK 99811-0801
  For information about Alaska travel and tourism

- **Legislative Affairs Agency**
  Division of Public Services
  130 Seward Street
  Suite 313
  Juneau, AK 99801-2197
  For information about Alaska's government

- **Alaska State Library**
  Historical Library
  PO Box 110571
  Juneau, AK 99811-0571
  For information about Alaska's history

Index

Page numbers in *italics* indicate illustrations.

Meet the Author

Donna Walsh Shepherd has lived in Alaska for twenty-five years and has visited every region of the state. Her home is in the forest at the base of the Chugach Mountains. Moose routinely step up onto her deck to eat from her flowerpots. She believes Alaska has two very special qualities—its invigorating beauty, and its generous people. During the writing of this book, she was delighted to experience so much of both, especially Alaska's Native people who so generously shared their histories and lives.

Many parts of this book came from her experiences traveling around the state. She has been very fortunate to tour the Pribilof Islands and the fur seal breeding beaches. At a wedding in Barrow, she ate traditional Native foods. While boating on Prince William Sound, a pod of killer whales swam alongside. When walking the streets of Juneau and Ketchikan in the rain, she saw rays of sun make the cities glisten. She learned much about the balance between land and industry touring the oil fields at Prudhoe Bay. And best of all, she has leaned far into the winds at the end of the Aleutian Islands while sea otters played in the green sea at her feet and bald eagles flew overhead.

Walsh Shepherd received her B.A. from Central Washington University in Washington state and an M.F.A. in creative writing from the University of Alaska. She has written many magazine and newspaper articles and several books for children including *The Aztecs, Uranus, Auroras: Light Show in the Night Sky, Tundra,* and *The Klondike Gold Rush.* She has won several regional and national awards for her writing. When not traveling and writing, she teaches at the University of Alaska.

Photo Credits

Photographs ©:

Alaska Division of Tourism: 117 bottom (ATMC), 127 (Rex Melton), 16 (Ernst Schnelder), 13

Alaska Stock Images: 24 (Anchorage Museum), 77, 83, 87, 113, 130 top (Chris Arend), 22 (Steve Armbrust), 41, 100 (Randy Brandon), 30, 132 top (Danny Daniels), 95 (Patrick Endres), 86 top (Al Grillo), 7 top center, 44 (George Herben), 109, 134 top (Mark Kelley), 72, 126 (Clark James Mishler), 70, 81, 101, 108 (Jeff Schultz), 116 (Gary Schultz), 7 top left (Michael Snively), 66 (Tom Soucek), 115 (Harry M. Walker)

AP/Wide World Photos: 117 top (Michael Caulfield), 107 (Ron Edmonds), 40

Corbis-Bettmann: 37, 38, 39, 86 bottom (UPI), 25

Envision: 105 (Steven Needham)

Gamma-Liaison, Inc.: 125 (Bill Roth)

Kobal Collection: 124 (Universal City Studios & AMBLIN)

North Wind Picture Archives: 15, 17, 19, 21, 135 bottom

Ron Levy: 7 bottom, 23, 34, 35, 45, 75, 88, 102, 106, 119, 122, 131 bottom, 134 bottom

Tony Stone Images: 7 top right, 103 (Chris Arend), 6 top center, 51, 110 (James Balog), 64 (Brett Baunton), 98 (Tom Bean), 12 (Wayne R. Bilenduke), 49 (Natalie Fobes), 6 top left, 6 bottom, 73, 74, 90 (Ken Graham), 9 (Fred Hirschmann), 111 (Cliff Hollenbeck), 76, 80, 118, 121, 135 top (Mark Kelley), 61 (Stephen Krasemann), 97 (Charles Krebs), 52, 133 bottom (R. G. K. Photography), 112 (Chip Porter), cover (Bill Ross), 94 (Mark Segal), 43, 96 (Nancy Simmerman), 67 (Paul Souders), 36 (Brian Stablyk), 65 (Robert Stahl), 48, 132 bottom (Michael Townsend), 2, 8, 131 top, 133 top (Larry Ulrich), back cover (Tom Walker), 6 top right, 58, 59, 60, 63, 91 (John Warden), 62 (Art Wolfe)

Yvette Cardozo: 26, 28, 31, 33, 46, 54, 56, 68, 79, 93, 130 bottom

Maps by XNR Productions, Inc.